AF326608

A PHILOSOPHY OF ART

A PHILOSOPHY OF ART:

IN LIGHT OF CLASSICAL PRINCIPLES

KEVIN WALL

SOLAS PRESS

2017

ISBN 978 1 893426 08 5

ebook ISBN 978 1 893426 07 8

Library of Congress Cataloging-in-Publication Data

Names: Wall, Kevin Albert, 1921-1988, author.
Title: A philosophy of art : in light of classical principles / KEVIN WALL.
Other titles: Classical philosophy of art
Description: Palo Alto : SOLAS PRESS, 2017. | Includes bibliographical
    references and index. | Originally published: A classical philosophy of
    art. Washington, D.C. : University Press of America, c1982.
Identifiers: LCCN 2017011397 | ISBN 9781893426085
Subjects: LCSH: Aesthetics. | Art--Philosophy. | Aristotle. | Thomas,
    Aquinas, Saint, 1225?-1274.
Classification: LCC BH39 .W28 2017 | DDC 700.1--dc23
LC record available at https://lccn.loc.gov/2017011397

ACKNOWLEDGMENTS

Writing is more a discipline than a pleasure, and, therefore, it requires motivation and a stimulus. There must always be those who encourage, help, and in many different ways contribute to it. I wish to acknowledge those who have done this for me: my colleagues at the Graduate Theological Union in Berkeley and my students there; and particularly the Dominican School of Philosophy and Theology. I wish also to acknowledge the helpful conversations I have had with Leo Daly in Mullingar, Ireland, whose knowledge of James Joyce encouraged me to add the final chapter to the text.

I was in Ireland designing a Celtic cross and, in conjunction with it, studying the techniques of ornamentation traditional to Irish carving and manuscript illumination. In my spare time, I made it a point to use the local library to satisfy myself concerning Joyce's knowledge of Thomistic aesthetics—at least to the extent that resources for this purpose were available. That led naturally to conversations with Leo Daly concerning Joyce.

My thanks also go to the Institute for Thomistic and Ecumenical Studies—a center under the sponsorship of the Dominican School of Philosophy and Theology—for providing not only a milieu in which my thoughts on aesthetics have been able to mature over the years, but also the financial support.

Kevin Wall OP   Berkeley 1982

TABLE OF CONTENTS

CHAPTER 1

Introduction

The purpose of this book is to present a philosophy of art faithful to the classical principles which are found in Aristotle and Thomas Aquinas. These principles, lead to an anthropology—a theory of knowledge, of will, and of sensibility—and to an understanding of the varieties of action possible to a human being as a consequence of this. Science (which I compact with philosophy) and morality and art are all affected by this anthropology. The concern of this book is to show the effect of this anthropology on the philosophy of art.

In brief, the result of this analysis will show that art, just as morality and science, begins in an imperfect self-consciousness and moves toward a perfect self-consciousness. Art is simply one of the ways of getting to this. It takes its sense from the fact that, as a human phenomenon, it must move away from the initial self-consciousness on a different path from that of morality or science, but must tend toward the same final end.

Thus, self-consciousness bathes the entire process and gives it radical unity, just as time gives radical unity to sense consciousness. Time, from this point of view, is to sense consciousness as self-consciousness is to rational consciousness or to the radical principle of unity for the human. This is a way of looking at art which is similar to the way in which Eric Voegelin has been looking at the philosophy of political science or the philosophy of history for many years; or Hans Georg Gadamer at the problem of hermeneutics. For both Voegelin and Gadamer a radical self-understanding is at both ends of the process.

At the moment, Voegelin is at work on a philosophy of self-consciousness which will make final sense of his previous thought. Central in this work is his notion of "anamnesis"—the remembrance of the past, which he feels is the inevitable means for the understanding of the self in the present. Although I agree in substance with this contention, my own purpose in this present work is not to attempt the same study in order fully to ground art in an adequate theory of self-consciousness, but rather only to show what the position and function of self-consciousness is for art, so that this might illuminate its significance for the total human spectrum of consciousness and action. In other words, I believe that the forgetting of the past has had serious consequences for the modern and contemporary understanding of art. In art, as in science and morality, to forget the total human experience—which is to forget history—is not to understand, or at least to cripple seriously, the possibility of understanding.

In art and morality, this has certainly been the case. But it is difficult to accuse science of such a massive forgetfulness—at least what we today call empirical science or simply science. Philosophy, which the Greeks thought primarily merited the term, has not been so judicious.

This philosophy of art should therefore be regarded as an attempt to understand aesthetic consciousness in terms of the full spectrum of the human past, present, and future. It is concerned with understanding art done now in the light of this whole, and not by the present alone.

Since 1982 is the centenary of the birth of James Joyce, I have chosen to add a concluding chapter on the debt of the great Irish writer to the aesthetic theories of Aquinas, such as he understood them. This is my tribute to his memory, and, it seems to me, a fitting way to terminate the book.

CHAPTER 2

The Nature of the Philosophy of Art

The philosophy of art is philosophical speculation about one specific human activity. As such, it presupposes a philosophy of all human activity—a philosophical anthropology. This, in the special philosophical tradition which is the matrix of the present discussion—the Aristotelian-Thomistic tradition—takes its significance from a natural understanding of God. Because of this, it designates the highest form of human knowledge to be theology. Such is the name which Aristotle gives to what we now commonly call "metaphysics." He designated it as *first philosophy* insofar as he thought it to be the heights of human insight; *wisdom* insofar as he considered it to be self-reflective and self-critical science; and *theology* insofar as he argued in it that the self-consciousness and self-love of *the* totally actualized being, that is God, is the root and explanation of everything else. For our particular purposes, it is the root and explanation of human artistic activity.

With this philosophical conviction, therefore, we do not primarily move from the lower to the higher, but from the higher to the lower. The lower we explain, to the extent that we can, in terms of what we understand of the higher. This does not mean that we do not induce from experience or from the concrete phenomena of the things which we study, but only that we do this within the matrix of a general understanding of the sense of the induction within the basic metaphysical insight into God. Without this basic metaphysical insight, the tradition holds, any induction lacks ultimate meaning. The things of nature have no ultimate sense or value.

That ultimate meaning is lacking is the consistent conclusion of contemporary philosophical doctrines of Irrationalism and Nihilism. Applied to human artistic activity, this means that it too would have no ultimate sense or value. The classical understanding repudiates this contention. Human artistic activity has ultimate meaning and value in the self-consciousness and self-love of God. It overflows from this, and seeks to return to it. It is thus one activity through which a human being seeks to return to God and thus shares in a special way in the quality of the terminal act in which the return is completed. The special quality of this terminal act which artistic activity has is that of possession and rest.

The philosophy of art, which has this understanding endeavors, therefore, to interpret the sense of artistic activity within the hierarchy of all created activity. One principle which it uses in this endeavor is that the higher operation is simpler, and the lower, more complex so that the lower divides up the simplicity of the higher. Its emanation is by way of complexification. The lower therefore has what the higher is. God, the highest, is existence and thinking and willing. Other things have existence and thought and will, or at least have existence and are objects of thought and volition.

This means, therefore, that one must first look to the spiritual world to determine how man falls off from the perfection of purely spiritual beings, and then, through him, explain the material world as falling off from his level of spiritual perfection. Thus purely spiritual being explains rational being and rational being explains matter. Thus, in this descent, sentient being explains the living and the living explains the lowest order of purely material being.

If this is so, then human artistic activity must be understandable in terms of the falling off of man from the "angel." Insofar as this is true of man, it is also true that the end of his activity must be to get as close to the level of activity of the "angel" as is possible for him. This indicates that one can answer the problem only by determining what the activity of the "angel" must be and how man falls off from this and how he tries to move toward it.

For the Thomistic tradition, the basic activity of the "angel" or the "separated spirit" of classical thought, Platonic, Neo-Platonic, and Aristotelian, is exhaustive knowledge and love of self. This is because, in that tradition, the essence of such a spirit is immediately present to its intellect and will, and both of these capacities are so proportioned to its intelligibility and desirability as to correspond exactly to them. Both faculties, therefore, in these fundamental acts exhaust the truth and the goodness of the essence.

Moreover, since that essence is not identical with its existence, its existence is not known immediately to it, but only mediately through the essence. That mediated knowledge shows the separated intellect that its essence is transcendentally related to existence, and the act of existence transcendentally related to it. In more modern terms, both relations are constitutive. Essence is what it is, therefore, through its entity-constituting relation to existence, and existence is what it is through its entity-constituting relation to essence.

This situation is self-negating and can be sustained only through a third relation to God. That third relation is therefore also seen through essence. This understanding is not inference, but mediated perception of reality, instantaneous and complete. Its limitation is the limitation of the medium, that is, the essence.

But the important point for our present purposes is that in this primary activity the pure spirit possesses its own essential intelligibility and therefore rests in self as an enjoyed content. This is also a rest in the possession of God to the extent to which the limitations of essence make this possible.

The philosophical significance of this for the tradition lies in its application of the principle of interpreting the lower level of being by the higher. Thus the pure spirit has essence-consciousness whereas God is essence-consciousness. This is the imitation of the divine by the creature. Thus, for God, intellection is intellection of intellection itself, but for the pure created spirit, intellection is of essence and then, by reflection of intellection. The pure spirit thinks primarily its own essential beingness and only secondarily its thinking of this. That is as close as it can come to the divine activity, and it is its essential share in the divine.

If now we think of man as being within the order of intellectual beings but lower than the order of the separated spirit, then we must interpret man's intellectual and volitional activity as deriving their significance ultimately from imitation of God, but more immediately from imitation of the knowledge and love of the separated spirit. So interpreted, man can be understood as potentially self-possessing at the beginning, and as moving toward full self-possession at the end. In more modern terminology, it is as if he were an intellectual being alienated from self-possession at the beginning and achieving it at the end. Thus, terminal self-possession becomes the sense of all of his activity. His thinking tends to this. His moral and practical activity of all sorts tends toward this. And, in particular, his artistic activity tends toward it.

Thus, morality, thought, and art all converge upon the same terminal goal, which must thus be the good, the true, and the beautiful at once. From this point of view, the activity of the separated spirit has thus, in self-possession, all the qualities of the moral, the contemplative, and the aesthetic. And therefore man, who is on the way to this goal, divides those qualities among different activities. Philosophical contemplation shares the quality of insight. Moral action shares the quality of possession of the good. Aesthetic activity shares the quality of rest. Human action must thus integrate these three to achieve partial completeness short of the goal. The tradition was sensitive to this. Virtue, it held, makes philosophical contemplation possible, and vice impedes it. And aesthetic activity fosters and enriches both.

The quality of insight which philosophical contemplation shares with final self-possession, contains the knowledge that the distance yet to be covered is infinite. This leaves it restless. Morality is similarly restless, since it is not brought to rest in the possession of the ultimate good. Aesthetic experience alone has the sense of rest of that possession, the sense of satisfaction and being at an end.

Thus, the scientist and the philosopher always sense the infinitely more which is to be learned of the subjects they study. And the moralist senses the character of means to an end in present moral activity. But the artist feels more the sense of rest and of coming to an end. There is nothing more in the work of art than what he has put into it. Therefore, nothing of its intelligibility escapes his grasp. In human experience, this is the only totally grasped content.

From the traditional point of view, therefore, this is the philosophical significance of artistic activity seen from the end toward which it is directed. Keeping this in mind, we may now proceed to study the origin and the genesis of the aesthetic.

CHAPTER 3

Origin and the Growth of Aesthetic Activity

Supposing that aesthetic activity is one of the paths through which a human being approaches the goal of total self-possession, and that this gives such activity ultimate sense, we have now to investigate inductively how it originates and how it develops. This means that we have to investigate the beginnings and the growth of that sort of human activity to which we commonly give the name of the "aesthetic." This name, which is modern and not traditional, designates it by the Greek word for sensation, which means that it sees it as especially connected with sensing. The classical names for the aesthetic are more helpful and more indicative of its true origin. This is especially true of the Greek word for it, which is "poetry." Aristotle points out that this name was given to signify that the "poet" is a maker. He makes meters.[1] Thus, the poet is a sort of maker, and, specifically, one who makes poetical lines. To understand him, we have, therefore, to understand what making is.

By the word, *making*, we commonly understand the sort of action which begins in the agent but terminates outside. The scholastics named this sort of action "transient." They opposed it to another sort of action which they named "immanent." This begins in the agent and terminates in the agent. In common language, which also makes this distinction, such an action is designated as "doing." And thus, common language distinguishes "doing" from "making" by the fact that the former both begins and terminates within the agent, but the latter, although it begins in the agent, terminates outside of him. The term is cut off from him. It is not a part of his being.

Thus, thinking is an immanent action and a doing because it begins in the person and terminates in the person. The object known—the thing expressed by the interior word—is part of the

---

[1] Aristotle, *On Poetry*, Chapter 1, 10, 1447b, 15

being of the knower. Although it is opposed to the knower relationally, the entire relation begins and terminates within the knower. This is true also of willing and choosing, and all such actions. But it is not true of making.

Making originates within the maker, but its opposite term is outside. So, for example, the house made by the carpenter is at the other end of the relation of causality, but it is also cut off from the being of the carpenter. The relation, as it were, passes out of his being into the being of something other than him.

Supposing this distinction and supposing also that the action of making is less radical than the action of doing, such that making follows from doing—one makes because one chooses to do so—and also that making is itself ordered to doing—one chooses to make in order to enjoy (an immanent action and itself a sort of doing), one can then understand the genesis of at least some types of art in the making of tools.

The making of tools is for the purpose of practical action of the transient sort. The axe is made to cut the tree. The bow and arrow are made to kill the deer. Note again that the supposition in both cases is that the agent knows the relationship between the tool and the desired end, and that he wills to make it for this purpose. And note also that the final end in each case is again the immanent one of doing—the enjoyment of the fruits achieved through the tool. Thus, doing, as it were, surrounds and grounds making.

But, for the moment, let us abstract from this broader context and consider only the constitution of the tool in itself. This is a relational structure, some of whose relations are intrinsic to the tool itself and one of which is extrinsic to it in the sense that it relates the tool to some effect outside of it. This extrinsic relation (the tool thus involves transient action) determines the intrinsic structure— the parts and their relations which constitute the tool.

Thus, the extrinsic relation of the axe is to cutting. The intrinsic nature of the parts—the quality of their materials—and their relations one to the other are determined by this. The axe head must support a sufficiently hard cutting edge. The addition of a handle—the adding on of another related part of likewise appropriate material—improves the control of the head in the cutting stroke and the power of the stroke itself. And the shape given both to the head and to the handle likewise improves or detracts from the performance of the axe. These improvements move the construction of the axe from the realm of pure craft to the realm of the aesthetic when they are such as to give the intrinsic relation of part to part a value in itself which the eye sees, independently of the practical value of better cutting. Seeing this, the eye then abstracts from the relation to the extrinsic purpose and considers merely the relations of part to part within the tool. It thus becomes an impractical relation to anything external.[2]

By abstracting from relation to use and considering only intrinsic relations of part to whole, we have reached beyond to the realm of doing and of contemplation. The contemplation is of the beautiful, that is to say, of the good of the intellect.[3] Since it is the good of the intellect, the intellect takes pleasure in it. And, by this pleasure, it recognizes that it has achieved its good.

What it has thereby achieved is insight into a part-to-whole relation within the object and without reference to something outside. This abstraction from such an extrinsic relation is thus the emergence of the perception of the whole (the aesthetic whole) of which the formerly practical parts now become aesthetic parts. And in this way the aesthetic emerges from craft, decoration from utility.

There are two further stages in this emergence. Before being pure decoration, the aesthetic seems to be first decoration within a useful tool. From this it then passes to the abstraction of pure decoration. But it then passes to a further and final stage in the restoration of the relation to something beyond. Only at this stage the reference is not to something extrinsic to the aesthetic, but to something intrinsic in it. The new relation, which restores the abstracted relation of practicality, now becomes that of meaning and presentation. This is intrinsic not in the sense that it constitutes the essence of the aesthetic, but in the sense that the aesthetic as such points to it, and therefore the one who contemplates the

---

[2] Ibid., I, 5, 4, first response.

[3] Ibid., I, II, 27, 1, third response. artistic activity may be above all to get to the meant content or the represented content through the aesthetic.

aesthetic sees this too. The one who makes the aesthetic may even have this as his prior concern, so that his concern in his artistic activity may be above all to get to the meant content or the represented through the aesthetic.

This final element is the one most difficult to adequately understand. This is above all clear when the very matter the artist works with is words, which have meaning and represent before they are incorporated into the aesthetic whole. The meaning and representation referred to above is precisely not this. That such is the case is evident from often reiterated statements of poets, such as Archibald MacLeish and Samuel Beckett, that a work of art means nothing, it is.[4] MacLeish says this of poetry in general and Beckett, in one use of the statement, of the work of James Joyce. *Finnegans Wake* and *Ulysses* seem to lack meaning but they are held to be great works of modern literature. Beckett defends them by asserting that such works do not have to point to a beyond, nor is it appropriate to ask: What do they mean? They mean nothing; they *are*. In other words, the essence of the essence of the aesthetic does not consist in the restored relation to the beyond, but in the intrinsic constitution of parts and whole within the artistic product itself.

This is to speak of the difficulty in the literary art. But it also exists in the plastic arts and was responsible for the Impressionist and particularly for the Abstractionist movements in modern art and all of the movements in contemporary and pre-contemporary modern art which seem particularly irrational. One can easily understand them in their historical context as an attempt to get away from the meaning-dominated art of the nineteenth century— to free art from meaning and thereby return it to the purely aesthetic. For all practical purposes, this is a return to "decoration" without reference.

Consequently, the portrait painter, for example, whose every stroke is dictated by realism or faithfulness to the face being painted, cripples the aesthetic impulse. The one who paints a

---

[4] See, *Our Exagmination Round His Factification for Incamination of Work in Progress* (London: Faber and Faber, 1972), p. 14

distorted face which hardly looks like a face or does not resemble one at all may really be trying to avoid this crippling effect and move back to the aesthetic—to that which, when seen, pleases and is therefore self-contained and self-validating. The highest achievement for the portrait painter would be to create a work of such a character that it forms an aesthetic whole independently of whether or not it is true to the model, but which also incorporates reference to the model as an added element. The great portraits in the history of art are great because of this added richness. Those which most hold to be poor are often so because, although they represent reality well, they fail in the aesthetic.

If what is true for the plastic arts can be universalized for all of the aesthetic arts, then they must all start in some practical action similar to the craftsmanship of making the tool, pass through the decoration within the tool stage, then into the abstracted decoration stage, and then terminate in the "decoration" with added reference or representation or imitation or mimesis. The number of different arts, in this aesthetic sense, will be equal to the number of different points of departure in practical making, and all of them will aim at the same term, which is the possession of self through making. They will all therefore be, terminally, a possession of self through a making of self.

The artist, perhaps naively but nevertheless correctly, speaks of art as self-expression. This says two things. From the point of view of the origin, it says that knowledge of the self already possessed, as it were, is thrown out as objective. It also says that knowledge of the self not yet attained is aimed at. This combines with the former to say that knowledge of the self, such as it now is, is the means to knowledge of the self such as it will be and is, in a mediate way, in the artistic production.

So the origin of art will always be in some sort of making with some sort of matter upon which the making works. And it will grow through a stage equivalent to the stage of decoration of the practical tool. And it will reach its first abstraction and the essence of the aesthetic in the decoration abstracted from the external useful end. When this is added again to the "decoration" in the form of representation or meaning or imitation or mimesis, the aesthetic will reach its highest form. From the same point of view, when the relation to the extrinsic useful end dominates or begins to dominate the determination of the parts within the aesthetic whole, art will corrupt.

Thus, the history of art will be this movement from practical beginnings to aesthetic heights to corruption through domination by reference to meaning or representation, and then to revival by return to decoration and, eventually, if the revival succeeds, to non-dominating representation and meaning. At the present moment, modern art seems to be in this intermediate stage. And one could argue about the works of James Joyce that they had returned to the decorative stage and then achieved this full perfection of meaning. At least, one could argue, this was his intention, as it well might have been, granted his acceptance of Aquinas' view of what art is.

CHAPTER 4

The Nature of the Aesthetic

From the considerations of the previous chapters, it becomes clear that the aesthetic object is essentially a complex of internal relations in sensible matter. These relations are of part to part and of part to whole. So there are aesthetic parts and an aesthetic whole, and these are bound together by relations.

The relations make the aesthetic object an object of reason, something which is intelligible. The sensible matter or the parts and the whole as sensible make the object an object in sense knowledge. Thus, in the sensed aesthetic object, reason sees intelligibility, but it is an intelligibility which cannot be removed from the object. It cannot be abstracted and seen in itself. Because of this, it cannot be universalized. Nor can it be conceptualized in the sense that conceptualization is abstraction, and seeing an intelligibility not as in this or that, but as in itself. For the same reason, the work of art cannot be conceived of as the incorporation of universal form in particular matter. The tool can be understood in this way—must be so understood. But not the work of art. One can therefore only point to it. One cannot explain why it is aesthetic.

For this same reason, one cannot teach a student how to produce a work of art as one can teach how to make a tool. For the tool, there is a universal why and how, but not for the work of art. The teacher can teach only how to originate the aesthetic work and how to manipulate or control the matter in which it is immanent. But the teacher cannot teach the aesthetic relations, which are as such only immanent in the work of art itself.

The fact that this cannot be done is itself indicative of the immanence of the relations in the aesthetic work and the impossibility of extricating them from it. The student must therefore see them in the given sensible and intelligible work of art, or place them in it, which is the same thing as saying *see them in it*.

This is what Aquinas means when he says that the aesthetic is that which, when seen, pleases, or that it is the good of the intellect or *a* good of the intellect. The intellect, when it sees the relation of part to part and of all parts to the whole, has the experience of attaining its object—the intelligible—and this causes it to come to rest in the object and to experience joy. The joy teaches the intellect that it has so come to rest. The artist is the one who can work a given material such as to reach this joy—this pleasure. The artist does so by choice, choosing the whole through the parts and the parts through the whole. This is why the Italian sculptors and artists in general speak of the progressive production of a work of art as a succession of many acts of choosing—*la scelta.* Choice, in this sense, cannot be taught. But the artist who makes it knows through the experience of intellectual joy that he is right.

In this way, in the work of art, the rational and the voluntary and the sensible or imaginative all combine in a special way. One can therefore say, supposing that this is so, that aesthetic activity is a capacity of reason—different from moral or speculative reason— but still a capacity of reason. It is therefore not an irrational activity nor is it an irrational product.

One can develop this further by observing that the production of the aesthetic is an activity of reason at its lower level, where it most closely approximates to imagination and the senses, and among the latter to hearing and sight. From this approximation, in fact, it takes its modern name of aesthetics. And from its approximation to imagination it most closely approximates, on the rational level, to mathematics. That is why mathematical reasoning is, of all universal reasoning, qualified by aesthetical terms. One speaks naturally of a geometrical or algebraic proof as elegant, and geometrical symmetry and pattern closely ally themselves to aesthetics, so much so that aesthetics seems often the extension of the mathematical into the sensed as such. This is most obviously the case when aesthetic productions take their point of departure in mathematical patterns and constructions, as in Celtic illuminations and decorations or in meter in poetry or in music.

Aesthetics is reason (plus will) at the lowest fringes of the use of this capacity. Aquinas maintained that theology, on the other hand, is on the higher fringe of the use of reason.[1] He meant, of course, revelatory theology, not the natural theology or the metaphysics of classical thought, which remain within the inner boundaries of reason. By this conviction, he expressed his understanding of reason as being a capacity to reach below its normal use and above its normal use. In the one case, it is sense knowledge which draws it and into which it extends itself, so that it becomes itself like the eye or the ear insofar as it is in them. In the other, it is divine knowledge which draws it and into which it again extends itself, so that reason becomes itself divine and thus thinks like God.

Thomas Mann's presentation of Dr. Leverkuhn in the *Dr. Faustus* has roots in classical thought. Leverkuhn is mathematician (rational within its normal sphere), theologian (rational at the upper fringe), and musician (rational at the lower fringe). Mann sees the continuity and interconnection of the three and exemplifies this in the life of Leverkuhn, the creative artist. And, as in the classical tradition, he sees the operations at either end of the spectrum as ecstasies and as demonic or at least subject to the demonic. The Greek would have said that the poet, just like the "theologian," is moved by the gods. They draw him out of himself, as it were. Or, actively, they "inspire" him and, passively, he is "inspired" or "enthusiastic." This occurs most naturally at the fringes of the use of reason, so Aquinas would claim, but also within the very boundaries of reason, although there it is not perceived so much as ecstasy.

Of course, the strong conviction of this tradition, which is also carried over in Mann's great novel, is that the ecstasy is truly an alienation from self and thus extra-rational or irrational. Aquinas does not want to conceive of it in this way. For him, it does not exceed the capacity of reason, but simply indicates the peculiar use of reason at its fringes.

But Mann agrees with Aquinas and Aristotle that the artist—specifically the author—is essentially a maker, not a thinker.[2] Aristotle holds that the very word in Greek indicates that this was

---

[1] *Summa Theologiae* I, 1, 9, first response.

[2] Thomas Mann, *Essays* (Vintage Books, K55, 1957), p. 303.

the common language conception. A poet is called a poet because he makes meters.

Thomas Mann also stresses the continuity of mathematics into music by relying upon Schönberg's atonal music and its mathematical basis for his analysis of the music of Leverkuhn. Leverkuhn, as it were, beginning in the normal rational world of mathematical ratios, extends reason down into the senses through analogous scales and an analogous construction of the scale. In this way, the musically aesthetic begins in reason in its normal use, and then reaches into aesthetics by pushing reason to its fringe use. That is like the illuminations in the *Book of Kells* which begin with geometrical patterns—that is within the rational in its normal use—and then move from this by the discovery of aesthetic parts within the aesthetic whole to the final work of art. This is similar to what Jay Hambridge proposed many years ago in his theory of dynamic symmetry. This begins with truly geometrical relations, not rectangular canvases chosen at random, and then moves on to the aesthetic. In a similar way, James Joyce begins with ordinary conversation or discourse, or ritualistic discourse and action, and then moves into the properly aesthetic.

This movement from the intermediate use of reason, or that use of reason which is usual and normal and from which any other must take its point of departure, can be described in another way. One can think of it as a use of reason in which it immediately confronts its object only mediately. Thus, in art and in theology, I confront the intelligible only mediately, whereas in science and mathematics and philosophy, I confront it immediately. Thus, art and theology are understandings *through* a medium, whereas science, mathematics, and philosophy are not.

Aquinas reasoned that this is because the aesthetic, in that it reaches down into sense knowledge and is, as it were, reason in eye and ear, has as its object a content whose intelligibility is so relatively weak in what constitutes the properly aesthetical that it cannot be seen directly in itself, as the many galaxies in the heavens can be seen only through the medium of the telescope and photography, since their luminosity is, relative to the eye, so weak. In a similar way, he held that the object of theology is blindingly intelligible so that, again, it cannot be looked at directly and therefore employs symbols or metaphors, and properly so.

I say *properly so* because I distinguish analogy from metaphor. From my point of view, metaphor is comparison on the way to analogy. And analogy is metaphor carried through to precision. When this is not done, thought remains ambiguous and nebulous so that the use of metaphor in teaching, although delightful in the beginning, is not the proper use of the relational, which, at root, both metaphor and analogy are. Thus, in science, mathematics, and philosophy, the use of the metaphor is a way in from which one must then escape. But, in art and theology, there is no escape. Both are properly metaphorical in the strict sense. And this is because the former is defective in the intelligibility of its object, whereas the latter is defective in the capacity of the knower.

The fact of defectiveness in the intelligibility of the object is manifested by the incapacity of reason to abstract the formal intelligibility from the aesthetic matrix and confront it itself. It cannot do this, but can only point to the work or put one in the presence of the work, and, at most, state one's conviction that it is a work of art—that it is good or beautiful.

Who can say why Beethoven's last five quartets are not only beautiful, but among the most sublime manifestations of the musician's art? What teacher taught Shakespeare how to write the soliloquy in the *Hamlet*? A teacher could expose Beethoven to great music or Shakespeare to great writing, but no teacher could tell them how to create great works of art or even unimportant works of art. The reason for this is obviously because the *how* is immanent in the work. It cannot be abstracted. I take this to be the reason why a writer or any artist many say "My work does not mean anything, it *is*!" In other words, its aesthetic intelligibility as such is immanent in it and cannot be removed from it. This is also the sense of Pope's judgment on Shakespeare that he brought no new thought to the world, but only superlative expression of fairly ordinary thought—"what oft was thought but ne'er so well expressed." Mann's remark that the author is a maker, not a thinker, says much the same thing, seen from the point of view of the genuinely aesthetical.

From the point of view of what is essentially the aesthetic in a work of art, sensible quantity and quality are the matter and the relation of part to part and of all parts to the whole, the form—the equivalent of the idea in scientific theory or in mathematics or in philosophy. Aesthetic perception is intuition of the whole as sustaining the aesthetic parts and of the parts as manifesting the whole. So, in music, one intuits the aesthetic relational whole whose basis is quantitative distinction and relation, and qualitative distinction and relation. The qualitative distinctions of the sounds and their relative sequence in time together with their similarity of dissimilarity in measure (the quantitative aspect of the sound)— these are the matter of musical art. And the total relationship of all of this to the immanent aesthetic whole—this is the form or the formal aspect.

The difference between this and the "meant," when meaning is added as part of the larger immanent whole in aesthetic consciousness (so that this is no longer an external relation to the work of art, but an internal although non-aesthetic factor), is clear from the fact that this meant can invariably be brought to the level of universal consciousness and thus discussed. One can thus discuss the meant content of Hamlet's soliloquy, but one cannot discuss what it is that makes the soliloquy an artistic success. To apprehend this, one must *say* it. The aesthetic as such is thus immanent in it.

It seems to me critical to make this distinction, since the growth or degeneration of a great tradition of art essentially depends upon it. When the meant factor overpowers the immanent aesthetic factor, poetry becomes didactic, and plastic art "realistic." One can then discuss the meaning of each of the parts because they are then parts of the meant rather than properly parts of the aesthetic. The aesthetic is, in fact, thus suppressed. This is what happened among the didactic poets of English literature and in Greco-Roman realistic art and in nineteenth century realism. Modern abstract art was simply a reaction against this, although, to the extent to which it refused by place to meaning in art, it was an over-reaction. The proper understanding of both and their success-ful combination is the supreme achievement of great art.

This is all the more important in that only through such a synthesis can certain meant contents be got at. To preclude the addition of meaning is to reduce art to decoration and exclude reason from access to a distinct world of intelligibility, distinct from but harmonious with the world of abstract rationality. One could argue, therefore, that this added element of meaning is really the end of the artist; that his joy in the immediately aesthetic as such is really only a medium to it. Moreover, as we saw in Chapter 2, the ultimate content of this meant factor is the intelligibility of the artist himself. Ultimately, therefore, he works at art only to get to himself, to possess himself and take joy of the possession. The Platonic vision of the meaning of the life of man resembles this. He is the fallen "angel" whose earthly life is a constant struggle to regain a pristine state of intuition of self and love of self. His science is a remembering of what was once known; his art is a recapturing of what was once possessed.

For this reason, the meaning factor brings into art not only what is a content of normal rational activity, but even what is above such activity. Here I think of John of the Cross in his famous mystical writings such as *The Spiritual Canticle* or the *Ascent of Mount Carmel* or the *Dark Night of the Soul.* In all of these, he uses the technique of beginning with poetry and then shifting to the normal universal use of reason. By the former, he points to the mystical experience so that it is seen in the poem through the medium of the aesthetic. In the latter, he discusses it theologically by the sort of theological insight which, although grounded in the upper fringe of the use of reason, properly develops in the normal. By this distinctive use of reason in two of its spheres, he attempts to get at and express the same objective reality—the mystical experience taken as object.

In the soliloquy of *Hamlet*—"To be or not to be"—we have a different level of meant content. The meant here is the properly rational of ordinary human experience. If this meant is simply exposed on that level, it seems banal. Death gives all humans pause. But, when this is seen through the joy-giving medium of the aesthetic—through what Shakespeare does with the words—it takes on a special allure and makes a special impression.

There are also those meant contents in art which are below this level—which have no clear meaning for us. We do not know the why. It is the weakly intelligible, at least relative to our minds. Such is the case with the human situation in general. Its sense is lacking to us. Simply to know this or to say it is unpleasant. But to say it or mediate it through the aesthetic is to give it the allure of the joyful. Insofar as the aesthetic has the meaning factor of this senselessness of human existence, it is unpleasant, but, insofar as it has the delightful factor of the aesthetic as such as medium, it is pleasant for us to contemplate. So we find joy in the *Hamlet* even though its ultimate meaning is that the rest is silence, and even though no philosophical or psychological analysis really removes the silence.

An experience similar to this is certainly communicated by Tolstoi's *War and Peace.* And Existentialists, such as Sartre and Marcel, can be seen as attempting to achieve the same effect through embodying philosophical thought in literary art—the drama. In the *Divine Comedy* Dante does as much for an essentially Thomistic framework of thought.

Thus, we have here three situations for the addition of meaning to the essentially aesthetic: that in which the meant cannot be brought down to the level of rational discourse, that in which it can, and that in which it cannot be brought up to the level of rational discourse. Art, as a medium, is a way of getting at all three, or at least of attempting to get at them. But in not one of these cases should the meant, so incorporated into the work of art, be considered as constituting its aesthetic aspect.

That is purely and simply the internal relations of part to part and parts to whole, immanent in the sensible matter. Thus, in the ballet, it is the relationship of movement to movement within the wholeness of the entire sequence of movements. In poetry, it is the relationships of sounds and length of sounds and numerical relationships of sounds within the aesthetic whole. And in prose, it is the same, without the added element of measure or feet or rhyme. And in sculpture, it is the relationships of part to part and of whole to whole within the aesthetic wholeness of the unique carved piece. In all cases, it is an immanent "idea" which cannot be either abstracted, universalized, or taught, but which can be *experienced.*

CHAPTER 5

The Properties of the Aesthetic

By properties in this discussion I will understand qualities which, although they do not belong to the essence and definition of the aesthetic, nevertheless follow from it. They are, in fact, only distinct from it in conceptualization. Really, they are therefore identical with it.

These properties, for classical aesthetics at least, have been held to be the following: integrity, harmony, and clarity. Sometimes the clarity is conceived of as the "radiance" of the aesthetic object. But this is again just another way of conceiving the same real thing.

The property of integrity means that the work of art contains all of the essential parts which it should. An aesthetic whole, lacking such a part, is therefore essentially defective. Lacking in less essential parts, it is less essentially defective.

The property of harmony means the parts genuinely relate to each other through the whole, that is they are truly parts of the given whole—not extraneous to it or without relation to it—and that they therefore have an aesthetic relation one to the other through this fact.

The property of clarity means that in possessing this the work of art is intelligible—clear, radiant—aesthetically. One sees clearly the whole and the essential parts. One takes joy in the vision.

Thus that which, speaking from the subjective point of view of vision, when seen pleases, and which, speaking from the objective point of view of content of object, is a whole immanent in sensible matter and seen only in it, from the point of view of its consequent qualities, is integral, harmonious, and clear.

We may add to this, from the point of view of the whole to which the parts relate, that the work of art is *one* and rooted in this one as in identity. I take that to be essentially what Aristotle was calling for in his demand for unity of time and place in the drama. This has been much discussed and much criticized. But, if it is understood as meaning that there must be, in the drama, an aesthetic whole and also, by the very nature of the meant in the drama, a meant whole, then it is simply pointing to unity and identity. A work of art which does not have these properties is not a diversity within unity, but a diversity without unity. The aesthetic whole, the most essential from this point of view—and the meant whole, the less essential—are missing. The work is therefore from both points of view defective.

Therefore a work of art which is not defective is one in which this is not true. The artist has discovered the whole! Or the artist has discovered one among many wholes which could be chosen, and has chosen one definitively. And he has then discovered its essential parts and, through this, harmonized them one with the other. Thus, discovery, choice, construction, and imposition are all involved, that is intuition, making, and embodiment of whole in the part.

The artist comes at these qualities through first working with what are only potential parts. Through these, by no process which can be taught, he sees a whole or wholes and chooses the one he wants. He then grounds the potential parts in the whole chosen as in their cause, and therefore the root of their aesthetic quality. This helps him to discover further parts and to decide to what extent to diversify them—how complex to make the aesthetic whole.

This is necessarily the artist's procedure and these are the choices and insights. He sees the whole through the possible parts, and then, through this insight, produces the remainder of the parts in their integrity. And, when all of them have been produced, he stops.

Thus, the artist proceeds in some ways in the inverse path to that of the scientist or the philosopher. He does not start with the thing of nature given and through its properties try to find out what it is and therefore why it has the properties. Rather, he starts with the ungiven work of art, the given matter potentially the actual work of art, and moves to determine what its properties will be and therefore what its "nature" will be. Thus, choice rather than necessity following from nature is the paradigm of his work. In this, he imitates the creativity of God, who, according to the tradition, chooses creation. Undoubtedly, this is why creativity is so naturally applied to artistic activity.

But there is a difference. The finite artist chooses the whole which he wants—the equivalent of the nature—and he is then determined as to the parts. God chooses the parts and through these the nature. In the choosing of God, there is no limitation. The classical insight did not accept the Deist theory of a God who chooses natures and is then committed to their operations. Rather, it conceived of the creativity of God as choosing operations and then choosing, because he is all wise, that sort of nature which will best support them. The finite artist, on the contrary, is limited to choosing the nature—the aesthetic whole—but is then necessitated as to the operation, the properties. And he is thus judged by whether or not the properties correspond to that initial choice of "nature," whereas God is limited in no way.

For this reason, the freedom of God is totally pervasive. All reality is as if it were a divine miracle. But the creativity of the artist is limited. He may choose the whole, but then will be judged by it and either praised or condemned. God chooses all. And nothing outside of his choice can be used to judge that choice.

In this way, the artist may be distinguished from the scientist, for whom, as I have mentioned, the properties of natures are given. It is not therefore for him to decide whether or not a stone will fall to earth if cast into the sky, but to observe what it does. But this is to characterize more the scientist as inducing from observation.

The scientist as theorizing upon induction resembles in some ways the artist, and this is coming more to the fore in the consciousness of philosophers of science and even of scientists themselves. For they know that they often have choices between theories with which to deal with the inductions and, to this extent at least, resemble the artist choosing his whole. More than this, they have also found that sometimes an apparently aesthetic choice concerning both theory and induction is useful and revelatory. Theoretical scientists now sometimes ask themselves: Wouldn't it be more beautiful is such and such were the case, and isn't such and such a theory more beautiful than another? When such aesthetic musings are then tested out, it is sometimes found that what seems to the scientist beautiful or more beautiful is in fact the inductive case or the more satisfying theory. Thus, there has arisen in the scientific community a sort of thrust toward aesthetic science.

It seems to me that this is indicative of the unity of the scientific and the aesthetic and akin to the unity of the scientific and the mathematical of which I have already spoken. But there is of course this difference in the unity—that the aesthetic supposition is governed not purely and simply by choice, in the case of the scientist, but by whether or not it corresponds to the data in observation or allows organization of the data, as in theory. These are the extrinsic norms which limit the choices of the scientist. No such norms limit the choice of the artist. He chooses a whole, and is to be judged by whether or not he successfully operates according to that choice, not by something outside of it. And he is to be judged only by someone who perceives the whole that has been chosen.

But there is another difference, again, between the scientist as choosing and the artist as choosing. The scientist cannot choose a closed system. It is always open to further induction, and theory must be tailored or adjusted to meet new facts. This is not the case of the artist. The parts of his whole, which may be compared to the data of the scientist, are finite. It is of their very essence that they come to an end. The artist often expresses this as "knowing when to stop." This knowledge grows with years and with experience. Often, it is acquired through testing by dropping parts. The skilled Japanese or Chinese brush painter does this. He makes a rapid sketch, places transparent paper on it, and alters it, continuing this process until the whole and the parts have emerged, and then he attempts to reduce the number of parts to the minimum. Obviously, they must be the essential ones, and none of these may be left out, or the drawing will lack integrity. But neither should they be more than the essential, for then the drawing is uncertain and overcharged, and the unnecessary parts cloud rather than reveal the whole.

Rembrandt, at the height of his power as a draftsman and an etcher, let alone as a painter, worked in this sense. Only so many strokes and lines as are necessary to capture the "effect." Velasquez has often been called the painter's painter because he could do this with infinite ease in an apparently slashing stroke of the brush. Such strokes are often called "suggestive," since they convey the desired impression with a minimum of complexity. They do not tediously overwork the part, but understate it, and yet to exactly the desired effect.

This ability to state with a minimum number of parts, so to speak, the wholeness of the aesthetic—this finitude of essential parts—contributes to the quality of possession and term, which art alone among human activities mirrors of the terminal quality of final self-possession. Because of this peculiar quality of art, it gives a sense of rest. One would not alter the five last quartets of Beethoven. When the Ninth Symphony terminates, there is the strong feeling of joy. This is it. It is all over. The rest is silence. Something has been finally and terminally possessed. This is the pleasure of viewing the rapid brush drawings of Rembrandt. In the interminable movement of life, this is a moment of rest.

Such, then, is a function of integrity in the work of art. It closes it off. The work has reached its end. There is not more to be said. The great artist and the perceptive viewer alike recognize this. They can see when an artist is too "busy" and they recognize that this is an imperfection. The imperfection gradually disappears as the artist advances in skill. As he does, the painter "cuts down" the palette. With fewer colors, he achieves the same effect. He recognizes in this that the excessive multiplication of sensible means to achieve an effect makes the work more difficult. It distracts from the essential. If the essential parts are not achieved, the whole is concealed, or even does not exist—has not been discovered and chosen definitively by the artist. He is then like an inferior craftsman who tries to overcome the basically non-aesthetic form of a glass vase by cluttering it up with cutting and etching.

That is why also combining mastery of color and mastery of design is so difficult in painting. To find the aesthetic whole in either and to reduce the parts to their essential minimum is difficult enough. But to do this for both in combination is to multiply the difficulty. Great painters thus tend to be either poor draftsmen or poor colorists. It is difficult to find one who is equally skilled at both.

In this same sense, J. W. N. Sullivan, with penetrating insight, points out that Beethoven was not at his best in opera, where one must bring the aesthetic out of drama, instrumental music, and vocal music all at once. He was greater in symphonic or inst-rumental music of that level, since the sensible parts from which the aesthetic whole must be drawn and into which only the essential parts must be introduced were less complex. And he was greatest of all when he reduced the complexity of the orchestra to the simplicity of the quartet. This was not an easy thing for him to do. Mozart's accomplishments made him draw back from it. And he did not acquire mastery of the quartet until later in his artistic career. But, when he did acquire it, he would write nothing else. It was the purest and most perfect vehicle for his great genius. With this simplified "palette" he could do anything. The last five quartets thus stand in the history of art as a unique achievement. Having mastered the quartet, Beethoven could do everything he wanted musically with it.[1] The rest then was, truly, silence.

This being so, it is clear that the integrity necessarily brings harmony. If all of the parts are truly parts of the given aesthetic whole, then they will necessarily aesthetically relate one to the other. In this relationship they will find unity in their diversity, that is in intelligibility. They will be perceived so to relate and they will be perceived to relate in completeness. That this should be called their harmony is easily understood. They are to each other as harmonious notes to the ear, that is to say, notes of different quality which blend. The mathematician discovers that those that do this have integral numerical relations one to the other. But that is not the essence of the aesthetic. In other words, that is not the relation of part to part which constitutes the aesthetic, but it has a certain resemblance to it and it is used for the purposes of the aesthetic. The aesthetic must please both the eye and the ear, or at least it should take into account that there is also this possibility and incorporate it into itself. Here again we see the kinship of the mathematical and the aesthetic—not an identity, but the kinship.

The consequence of this is, the work of art lucidly reveals the whole and the parts in the complex interrelations. It thus has clarity or radiance. From the analysis being made here, it is clear that this clarity is not the reasonableness of the added factor of the meant,

---

[1] J. W. N. Sullivan, *Beethoven: His Spiritual Development* (Mentor Books: 1948), pp. 123-44.

but the lucidity of the properly aesthetic intelligibility. Because of this, what cannot be universalized and thus abstracted from the work of art to be considered in *itself*, is nevertheless clearly seen in the concrete work. This clarity of visibility is a pleasure for the intellect, just as clear seeing is a pleasure for the eye. And lack of insight and lack of vision are unpleasant for the intellect and the eye, respectively. The intellect flees ignorance and the eye darkness. The intellect seeks to know and the eye to see. Thus, Aristotle can say that men first began to philosophize because they fled ignorance, and therefore because they were conscious of it and unhappy with the consciousness. For the intellect, therefore, knowledge is a good, and clear knowledge a greater good, and perfect knowledge the greatest good. A work of art must therefore possess the clarity described, because when seen it pleases, that is to say it is the good of the intellect.

These therefore are the radical "properties" of the aesthetic whole. It must be integral, harmonious, and clear. We must now discuss in some detail the artistic process by which the artist produces such a work.

CHAPTER 6

The Creative Process

Given that a work of art is a immanent tissue of relations of part to part and of all parts to the whole; also that the parts are finite so as to form a closed system, and that the properties of this system are those of integrity, harmony, and clarity. The question arises how does one produce the work of art? For the artist, as maker, produces it.

This, as we have also seen, involves a given—the matter upon which the artist works which is essentially accessible to the senses, especially sight and hearing. But, of course, the imagination too is working along with these external senses; and also choice, which must determine the aesthetic whole, naturally by way of preference among many possible ones.

Taking these as the subjective point of departure, the painter will begin to draw, perhaps with some natural object as a suggestive point of departure. The size of the paper or the canvas enters into consideration. The lines and the areas must relate to that. The painter has a simple way of stating this: the sketch must "fill the space." It must be a sketch within the space and taking it essentially into account. Thus, positioning is crucial.

As the artist begins to draw, tentatively, the potentially aesthetic parts may be laid down, but at this point they are not actually the aesthetic parts as such. They are, nevertheless, related one to the other in a probing search for the whole to which they must relate and through which they will have their aesthetic interrelations. If the drawing is successful, at some point the whole is seen and is chosen. Imagination, memory, choice, and insight all function here. Imagination can "visualize" a line or an area if memory causes it to do so. Imagination visualizes one or another line stressed or one or another line suppressed, and the hand then responds, moved by a choice as yet not actually having chosen the aesthetic whole.

At a sudden point in the process, insight sees *a whole*. It emerges immanent in the sketch and relative to it. Certain lines come to the fore and others recede or are eliminated in imagination, and other lines again are added because the whole shows that they should be and imagination represents them in this way. At this point, the artist removes or adds. As this is done, the whole begins to emerge more clearly in the work, and he is able to test it out for its value, that is determine whether this is what is wanted. It also suggests through imagination other wholes closely or not so closely related to it. If the artist decides that the emerging whole is not itself the one wanted, he may destroy the sketch and start afresh, or, as the Japanese brush master, place a second piece of transparent paper upon it and alter it to a different aesthetic whole and parts.

Proceeding in this way, he gradually develops the integrity of the parts, dropping those which are relatively nonessential and aiming at achieving the desired effect with the fewest parts possible so that, by their very simplicity, they will reveal whether any crucial and essential part is lacking and must be supplied. When this process has been carried through to completion so that the aesthetic whole and only the essential parts are present, and these in their integrity so that they form a closed structure with the whole, he stops.

If the resultant work of art has purely decorative value, then this is all. But if it also intends to imitate or represent something other than itself—as in the portrait—then another condition is added. Each aesthetic part must then function not only as a part of the aesthetic immanent whole, but also must "represent" the extra-aesthetic object, and function as a part of it too. A double function is therefore imposed upon them and upon the aesthetic whole.

When this is the case, the artist must work back and forth between these two poles. Representation, of more or less exactitude, must govern his choices, but they must be, at the same time, as if they had no representative, but only an aesthetic function. In this case, the artist works first toward representation and then attempts to rework the representative parts so as to form an aesthetic whole.

Such parts must therefore be both necessary for representation and necessary or essential for the integrity of the aesthetic whole. The artist must, therefore, discover such a whole and such parts. In the case of a portrait, when the representative parts are exact but the aesthetic parts as such and the aesthetic whole are lacking, one calls the work "photographic" or "academic," meaning in both cases something aesthetically pejorative.

In saying this, I abstract from the case when a photograph itself is a work of art. There the photographer has made the representative parts function also as aesthetic, and has made the photograph one in which an aesthetic whole is immanent such that it has its own being independently of its realistic truth as representation or even a quality of decoration in an abstraction.

Thus the stages in the artistic creative process are these:

1. the *free working* of a material which produces alterations and potentially aesthetic parts of an aesthetic whole without insight into that whole; or the externally governed working of a material with a view to representation and then its free working with a view to discovering the coalescence of the aesthetic parts and whole with the representative parts and whole;

2. the *discovery* of (and therefore insight into) the aesthetic whole, and,

3. the *determination and imposition* through this insight of the essential aesthetic parts in their integrity such as to close off, aesthetically, the work of art.

It is useful, at this point, to compare this process with the general working of reason and the senses to see the similarities and differences in artistic and speculative activity.

In both speculative and artistic spheres, reason works inductively (in the classical Third Figure of the syllogism)[1]; moves

---

[1] Editor's Note: We owe the first formal study of deductive, syllogistic reasoning to Aristotle. In the *classic* development of the syllogism there are three propositions, the two premises and the conclusion, and there are three *figures* defined by the arrangement of terms in the propositions. If the middle term, which occurs in both premises, is the subject in one premise and the predicate in the other, then the syllogism

then by comparison, in the case of speculation, and by tentative relating and aesthetic insight in the case of art, to theory (in the classical Second Figure of the syllogism); and finally, in the case of speculation, grounds the induction of properties in theory, and, in the case of art, adds the properties or confers them upon the work (in the classical First Figure of the syllogism). Thus, whereas speculation sees insight as the ground of property, art, through insight, creates property.

This situation differs for mathematics and empirical science. Mathematics proceeds from insight into figures—the nature of the circle, for example (in the Second Figure)—to the construction of properties (in the Third Figure); to the grounding of the constructions in insight (in the First Figure) through which conceptual properties are then had. Thus, geometry proceeds from the insight into the nature of the right-angled triangle (Second Figure and definition) to the construction of squares which have the sides of the triangle as common parts with it (Third Figure); to the grounding of the conceptual property; that the sum of the squares on the sides other than the hypotenuse is equal to the square on the hypotenuse, which grounding is through comparison and similarity (Second Figure) and rooted in the nature of the right-angled triangle. Thus, geometry, in this case, passes from the Second Figure into the Third, and, through passing back into the Second, into the First.

Empirical science, on the other hand, and, in its own way, philosophy in the genesis as classically understood, begins with the Third Figure, i.e., sees universal properties through it; then passes to the Second Figure, that is compares its subject of investigation with others of similar properties to arrive at a tentative insight into its nature; and then passes into the First Figure to ground the properties in that insight.

Art resembles empirical science in that it begins an "induction" in the Third Figure and then passes into insight in the Second. But it then resembles mathematics in that it next goes back to the Third Figure to "construct" the aesthetic parts, and only then to the First

---

is, said to be, in the first figure. If the middle term is predicate in both premises, the syllogism is in the second figure. If the middle term is subject in both premises, the syllogism is in the third figure.

clear and striking. Multiplication of adverbs and adjectives is often an endeavor to remedy a basically poorly phrased sentence. It is, as I have already said, like cutting and etching a glass decanter whose basic shape is an aesthetic failure.

These remarks are true for the beginning of a creative work—*for getting into it*. Simplify the means so as to confront directly the aesthetic task and maintain freedom even under the pressure of representation. If this is done, then the beginning is appropriate. And, if one has the ability, aesthetic insight will occur. At that point, a different difficulty emerges: that of finding the truly essential parts of the aesthetic whole and of knowing when to stop, which is to say, the problem of finding all of them so that the work has integrity. Harmony and clarity will immediately follow.

Just as in beginning, this procedure too requires discipline. There is not only the proper way in and the proper way to continue, but the disciplining of oneself in both instances. Aesthetic insight cannot be taught, but discipline can. And, without it, aesthetic insight is fruitless.

The writer must learn to cover a number of sheets every day. The painter must learn to cover a certain amount of canvas. The sculptor must patiently take up the chisel. This is the discipline. But each true artist knows that, once he submits to it, he will soon experience aesthetic insight and that this will then provide the energy for the carrying out of the work. The joy of the beautiful is stimulating. It is, in fact, the source of the energy from which all art emerges.

That energy is immediately possessed in the present work of art insofar as it is aesthetic and thus pleases, and by this draws one to artistic activity. In this, the discipline and the difficulty of entrance and the even greater difficulty in carrying through to the end is recompensed by the joy of the end. Balzac's magnificent description of this process in *Cousine Bette* can hardly be improved on. The abyss between conception (aesthetic insight into the whole sufficient to enable one to determine the parts, but without yet determining them) and execution (the pains, the agony, the patience required).

But what draws one ultimately more than anything else is that this is a way to self-possession. It, like the Ideal of Pure Reason, which for Kant made speculative thought possible by providing the end without which it could not exist— that ideal also which is the ego, makes artistic activity ultimately possible, whether the artist concretely realizes this or not. Regardless of this, and not through his choice but through his nature, he must seek self-possession, just as morally he has no choice but to seek happiness, and, speculatively, total insight into self. All of these movements thus terminate in the same final goal, which is therefore the ultimate energy which draws them.

Moreover, since in perfect self-possession the human person, just as the "angel," knows himself not to be God and to be dependent upon God as a principle of being and sustenance, this final goal is also at the same time theological. That this is the case for metaphysics Aristotle clearly indicated when he called it "theology." Contrary to Heidegger, he would maintain that there is no insight into being which does not immediately terminate in God and take all of its sense from what is in his known of him in that termination. Thus, Kant also made the "ideal of God" the ultimate teleological principle practical analysis of the dynamism of knowledge in the *Critique of Pure Reason*. In carrying this analysis farther and in removing some of its contradictions, Hegel, as Maréchal, perceptively understood him, was on his way to rejoin the classical analysis of the situation. As the culmination of German Idealism, so-called, he was therefore the most comprehensive and penetrating manifestation of this thrust.

Thus, creative artistic activity is at term not only self-possessive, but also theological. And it is therefore in its intermediate stages partially self- possessive and partially insight into divinity.

CHAPTER 7

Symbol in the Creative Process

The considerations of the preceding chapter concerning the creative process need amplification chiefly from the point of view of symbol. This is because, as we have seen, although representation of what lies beyond the aesthetic whole and its parts is not as such intrinsic to them, nevertheless it can be added, and, from the point of view of what art is trying to get at, must be added. This is especially urgent if one holds that art is a means to ultimate self-possession and that its purpose here and now is to afford an intermediate and imperfect self-possession.

Thus, the creative process is both active and passive. In it, artists "express" themselves—a way of speaking which would seem to indicate that they already in some degree possess themselves and project this initial possession in the work of art. But more radical than this active factor of projecting self, is the passive one of being drawn by the full possession of self. This is the fundamental cause of artistic activity, which thus becomes more a being drawn to than a making or taking possession of. Artists instinctively refer to this when they speak of being seized upon by an idea and being caught up in the fury of aesthetic activity.

There is the demonic in this, as Thomas Mann argues in *Dr. Faustus.* It is as if someone outside of the artists—or some force—inspires, forces, and impels them. And this seems to them to be an action psyche from a raging power. The impression that this is so is all the stronger because artists, caught up in the improvisation which initiates the creative process, suddenly feel that energy is being poured into them which otherwise they do not seem to have. When they are not under the spell of this impulsion, they need to drive themselves to work and thus sense resistance and the need for discipline. But this disappears when, through discipline, they make themselves work the material and when, in the course of this, they intuit the aesthetic whole. The intuition seems to infuse them with enthusiasm and strength. In virtue of this, they do what otherwise they feel they cannot do. They will then put hours into artistic activity and perform marvels of physical strength—one thinks of the work of a great sculptor carving marble or granite—and show surprising patience and endurance. In all of this they seem to be caught up in a rapture—to be possessed. This someone else is really the artist's own being as terminally possessive, but now working as an end and, as such, irresistibly attracting. This unpossessed but possessible self is the demon and it has the energy.

Artists, who are aware that this process will occur when they get into the work, however they may articulate its meaning and however they understand it, know that they have only, through discipline, to begin in order to have the phenomenon occur. They therefore have no hesitation to start the process because of their lack energy at the beginning. The process itself, they know, will remedy this defect and it will be self-sustaining, self-validating, enjoyable.

This being so, they are not discouraged by the fact that what they do will perhaps perish. The acidity of the Athenian air will dissolve the Parthenon. A deranged mind will slash the Rembrandt canvas or damage the Pieta. But nothing of this sort will ever affect the partial possession of the goal that the production of the great works afforded the artists. This production, temporal from the point of view of its sensible matter, is eternal from the point of view of the immortal soul which is responsible for it. Even the viewers who truly apprehend its beauty will say that this is so for them. Through it they too possess something of themselves—know, one often says, what it is to be a human being; know the greatness of humanity. It is this subjective seeing which is the real immortality of art and which, in fact, reveals also the immortality of the person.

All of this is given through relation to the "meant" which artists embody in their work, which meant is the self partly possessed but also seen dimly beyond as the fully possessible and, as such, drawing the artist on. This is where the aspect of symbol, or sign, or metaphor enters in. As it does, the work of art becomes similar to human words to which meanings are arbitrarily attached. Such meanings become internal in the understanding of the sign. To understand the word is not merely to hear it, but to apprehend its relationality. This means that the relationality, as such, is in the one who understands. Both the beginning—the sound—and its relation to the meant are in the knower. Through that, the meant thing is in the knower. And, since it is in the knower as immanent in consciousness, it *is* the knower—part of the knower's being.

But there is this difference, as we have already argued although in a somewhat different way: the meant thing which is in the knower through words—through discourse and interpretation—is separable from the words. The knower can think such things in themselves and without reference to particular words or even without reference to any words at all. We have, after all, understood contents for which we have no words, at least in common language, and which we cannot therefore express in common language. I think here of the remark of Aquinas: that we have no word for the effect in the will as loving which is akin to the effect in the intellect as thinking to which we give the name "interior word." For him, this effect exists, but is not named.

However this may be, the meant in art is not separable from the art which means it. For this reason, it cannot, in its proper character as "mediated" through the aesthetic, be separated from the aesthetic. One can only see it in the aesthetic sign and, to communicate this, one can only point. We will deal later with the implications of this for art criticism. For the moment, let us only concern ourselves with its implications for the understanding of how the symbol relates to art or how art becomes and is—although not always—symbolic.

Add to this the consideration, that the immediately symbolized content may itself symbolize something beyond—even many concatenated relations to a series of beyonds. And it must, by its very nature, always point to that beyond which is total self-possession. To make a comparison, just as all conceptual contents point to being, ultimately; and are simply restrictions of being such that being is "that which first comes into the intellect," so one can say that all art products, when they have meaning, point ultimately to the meant, which is the self totally possessed, and that they are all simply partial realizations of this possession.

Let me add here, in passing—we will take it up later in more detail—that the symbol, as we are describing it, causes something to be in the mind—the human mind. The being of such a thing is therefore "being in the mind" or "being understood"—the *esse est percipi* of Berkeley has a familiar ring here and relates to this. But if this making to be in the mind through relation were also making to be really through relation, then symbolization would be realization and it would be divine creative activity, but also, subordinate to this, divine sacramental activity.

This remark is important in the understanding of James Joyce and what he is about in *Ulysses* and *Finnegans Wake;* as well as in the understanding, it appears to me, of what Heidegger is about in his later works when he thematizes that the word makes being. It seems to me that both of these authors are conscious of and recall the sacramentality of the Roman Catholic Church from which they took their early roots, and that both of them exploit this consciousness for their own purposes, although in different ways. Joyce takes the *signum efficax*—the efficacious sign of the Roman Catholic tradition, that is the sort of sign which not only indicates something other than itself, but, by indicating it, brings it into being—most seriously. For this reason, he can be understood as attempting to make art do this and, in doing it, fulfill the expectations of the sacrament; to save, in whatever sense salvation is conceived.

Sign or symbol—and I do not want here to make the distinctions which are often made today for purposes which are not those which I have in mind—I take to be something other than—*really* other than the thing signified. And I take signification to be a relation. The sign has the relation, and by it points to something other than itself. A word, which is a sound or a combination of sounds, by arbitrary convention points to something really distinct from itself. Smoke, which is the effect of a fire, "points to" to presence of fire because it also has a relation to it, although this case is not through mere convention and choice.

If the work of art is also to contain elements of the symbolic, then we have to decide in what way. We have to decide this in the matrix of a theory that such pointing beyond is extra-aesthetic and that it is therefore added to the aesthetic and does not constitute it. This being so, we therefore deliberately add to the aesthetic parts that they must also bear the burden of symbolizing something beyond, somewhat in the way in which a word symbolizes an object. The adding of this burden obviously complicates the task of the artist. He must give his work only those elements which are truly part of its aesthetic wholeness—therefore make it integral and finite and closed—and, at the same time, must make such elements significant.

Are they to be made significant in the sense that the artist tells the viewer or the listener that this is what the parts mean, and so, fashion a sort of private language and make the viewer or listener agree to it or at least come to understand it? Or are they to be significant because they have the relationship of likeness to an object, as in a portrait which images a face? Or should one push this even further and say that the parts are like the smoke which signifies fire—hardly a likely hypothesis, since this would then make the object the creator of the parts, rather than the artist? Or could one be so daring as to invert even this and say that the artist, by making the "smoke," makes the fire? The resemblance between this and the conception of Heidegger for language and of Joyce for artistry in language is striking.

If we reject as entirely absurd the thesis that artists create the meant and therefore presuppose that it has its existence independently of their creative activity, then we are forced to conclude that they can only signify it by arbitrary convention, as words do, or that they can signify it only by representation or likeness or image; by all of which I mean the same thing.

Of course, signification through convention does occur in what we customarily refer to as art, especially in religious art. Thus, we are accustomed to taking a halo as indicating sanctity. This acceptance is close to that which gives words meaning. It involves the conventional—the agreed upon. Everyone will accept, within the community for which the acceptance is valid, that this indicates sanctity. By accepting this indication, the community creates its own sort of religious language. This is therefore one sort of significance or meaning which is added to art. But, it bears repeating again, the addition must be such that the added part is, independently of its accepted significance, an aesthetic part of the whole. If it is not, then it is a rational, non-aesthetic addition which destroys the integrity of the artistic achievement as such, or, if it does not entirely destroy this, enters in as an alien element. The halo that is not there because the immanent aesthetic whole permits or demands it, but it is there because the artist has decided to transgress the boundaries of the aesthetic, introduces an alien element.

One question which these considerations introduce: is whether aside from such signifying elements added to art, art would exist at all? Another is this: are there secular, nonreligious symbols which can function is somewhat the same way? I am speaking in this context of the immediate work of art, since I have already argued that the ultimate relationality in the signified content is to the self and to God, so that neither can really be removed, however much the artists may think that they are doing this and however much they may want to do so.

These questions are certainly important, since many historians and critics of art have observed that, where sacramentality disappears, art disappears. There are those who point out, rightly or wrongly, that, with the Reformation and the iconoclasm which it introduced and its anti-sacramentalism, religious art disappeared. And there are those who argue, in this same sociological context, that the religious is the root of everything else: culture, civilization, science, and art.

But the value of this argument may simply be that artists lose heart when the religious is removed or, at least, lose their roots. This may point to a psychological effect rather than to the *de jure* of art and artistic activity. That psychological effect might be roughly the same as the effect upon the scientists who discover that the results of their work are, even in the short run, a great evil for the human race, and possibly an even greater evil in the long run. Convinced of this, scientists may well lose heart and no longer find the tedious work of the laboratory enticing.

Viewing this from the historical point of view, one can say that the Egyptians, who maintained in their art close relations with religion and culture, never lost their formalism. But they were great artists who worked in a cultural and religious context which imposed certain rigid rules upon them, whose nature they understood and whose regulations they willingly accepted. But even under these restraints they could do with stone—even the hardest stone, since they worked granite—and wood, and precious metals what the artists of Greece did who learned from them. But, unlike the Grecian artists, they never cut themselves off from their religious and cultural roots. The Greeks did this, and their art then degenerated into Greco-Roman realism. Dawson, reflecting upon this, argues that Hellenism never died as a possibility and an ideal of humanity, but only as an actuality, since it undercut its cultural roots. The agrarian culture which supported these moved to the city, and Hellenism—the great Hellenism of Plato and Aristotle and the dramatists and poets and sculptors—withered.

But, I repeat, this is to argue concerning the psychological and cultural roots of artistic productivity. If they are rooted in religion, then when religion fails, they fail. When religion "gets a cold," they "get pneumonia." And this may well be the explanation of why art failed in the post-Reformation period to the extent that this was iconoclastic and why therefore Rembrandt should not be looked upon as a proof of the contrary, but as a last vestige of medievalism.

My concern here is not with the cultural and psychological factors which make an artist work—the environment which stimulated Michelangelo and Beethoven, but with the inner stimulus in art itself which can be abstracted from these and which must be abstracted in order to understand it in itself and in its own essential principles. To make this statement more concrete, I refer again to J. W. N. Sullivan's analysis of the artistic growth of Beethoven, who by the very circumstances of his life was forced to make such an abstraction. He lost his hearing, nearly entirely, and contemplated suicide. When he managed to pull through this traumatic experience, which he surely never would have chosen for himself had he known that it would be his fate, he then produced music simply because he was drawn by the aesthetic and could not resist the pull. Cultural supports, popular acclaim, and immediate understanding and approval then lost all meaning for him. He composed because he had to compose. And, when he did this, he produced his greatest works. His last five quartets are a unique phenomenon in all art history. And his whole psychology, both in producing these transcendent words and in presenting them for public performance, was totally different from his psychology when he began his brilliant career. I agree with Sullivan that this fact may be unique in the development of any artistic talent, even the incredible talent of Shakespeare in the dramatic art.

But my concern with this, is the abstraction which Beethoven's late work reveals and which manifests the essence of the aesthetic. I want to get at the function of the symbolic, the significant or the meaning mediating factor when this is added to the work of art. I think here of the third movement of the Beethoven quartet no. 15, op. 132, in A minor, which he entitles a "thanksgiving—a holy thanksgiving—to God for the restoration of his health, and which he couches in the Gregorian Lydian mode (going back to the medieval musical tradition as well as the Greek, as if this were the appropriate way to express the sentiment). He divides this into two parts, each with a different quality of passion, the first being that of the adagio, or the gentle and slow, and the second, that of the andante (*neue Kraft fuhlend*,—"feeling new strength"), which obviously suggests the slowness of the passions in sickness and the stirring of movement as recovery begins. Here the subjective passion is the medium through which the objective reference is made, or is, at least, a medium. One speaks and moves slowly when one is tired. One begins to move with animation as strength returns. This is a sort of "smoke" and "fire" relationality. At least in the andante, the "smoke" is the stirring of life for which Beethoven is grateful to God.

Of course, this may seem contradictory to what I have said already about seeking abstraction from the religious as such. After all, the quartet is deliberately religious in inspiration. But it here rejoins the ultimate purpose of all art, as well as all human activity which we have already considered. It is all theological, but not necessarily religious in the sense of the approach to God through a religious sacramental community with set ways of acting. Beethoven has abstracted from this aesthetically and has simply recognized that music is, for him, the way of saying should nevertheless choose the "religious" Lydian mode, whose origin was historical. This means only, that he recognizes that this approach was a choice of genius in the tradition. He integrates it so perfectly into the quartet that it is as if it had no history.

It is often said that Beethoven's achievement in this quartet, and in all of the great five, transcends the possibilities of music. This is an Eckhartian way of saying that, within that sphere, it achieves so much that it is as if it went beyond it. This is also often said of Rembrandt's "hundred guilder print" of Christ preaching to the beggars. Artists so esteem this that they want to say it is unique: that it transcends the medium. Of course, neither transcends the medium, but simply shows that the transcendent is contained in the medium. Of course, few attain it to this extent. Art points to the transcendent, and the greatest art is that which does this pre-eminently.

If this is so, then the comparison of Beethoven's realization with that of Rembrandt is highly suggestive. Beethoven uses human moods of slowness and agitation as symbolic of sickness and recovery, and the religious mood of the Lydian mode as symbolic of reference to God as cause. The former is like "smoke" to "fire." Sickness causes slowness, and health, quick movement. Thus, the passivity of sickness and the activity of returning health are taken as symbols of the action of God—the permission and the active intervention.

Rembrandt's symbolism, on the other hand, is not that of effect to cause, but that of image to reality. The Christ, with his hand extended, is an image of the real Christ. In this image, light and shade are so disposed that even if the etching did not resemble or represent a real scene; the interrelation of its parts is that of aesthetic parts to an aesthetic whole, and the parts are finite, reduced to a minimum and essential. Yet they carry the burden of the aesthetic and, at the same time, of the representational.

Thus, Rembrandt uses the "similar to the objective" as his symbolic medium, and Beethoven, the "subjective stirrings of the soul" as his. But, in both cases, the sequence of the sounds and the disposition of light and shadow stand as if they were values in themselves; the added reference.

It is interesting that, in both of these cases, there is a sort of confession of faith. The viewer need not understand the confession in order to appreciate the work. But for the creator, however, it is certainly crucial to the production of the work. Beethoven was motivated by the desire to possess God as the object of thanksgiving, and Rembrandt, Christ as the root of his understanding of himself and his art. Both understood their art as means to these ends which are, at root, the same. And I would strongly urge, that even one who does not share the motivation of the artist picks it up as the ultimate sense. No one who listens to Beethoven's quartet, even though he does not share his faith, can doubt what that faith was and, to the extent that he loves the work, love it too as the cause of the work. And no one who sees the "hundred guilder print" can fail to extend his love to the faith object of Rembrandt, at least as motive of the work. He may think one deluded in his belief, but he must think that the belief has to be marvelous to motivate such works, and its object, marvelous to motivate the beliefs.

This still leaves us with the problem as to whether the relations of significance involved are rational, as in words, or real, as in representation. If they are real, as in representation, as, for example, in a portrait, the artist need not explain or assert the meaning. But, if they are rational, as in words, then he has to tell the viewer or the listener what these private words mean. He has, of course, some help if the immediate means is subjective emotion, as in the Beethoven quartet of which we have just spoken. The relation of this to the object signified is, in the tradition, real. The tradition understood this relation as intentional, and Husserl, following Brentano, and Heidegger, following Husserl, picked this up from the tradition. This is the real relation of the knower to the known and of the lover to the beloved, which relation, from this point of view, is at once action and relation and quality. The reverse relation from the object to the knower and the lover is, in the tradition, rational, not real. Charles Hartshoren found this a fascinating distinction and was surprised at its sophistication and that it was in the tradition and had been forgotten.

This leaves us with the conclusion that the relationship which is added to the aesthetic and which is most commonly spoken of as its "meaning" shares something of the nature of a real relation, as of smoke to fire, or thought and love to their objects, and something of the nature of a fictitious and conventional relation, as of words to what they signify. The "symbol" in art must therefore bear all of these resemblances. But it must also differ from the word in that it is not a universal symbol and therefore does not enter into the realm of public discourse. It does not do this because it is not the exemplification of universal, but a unique product. This is why it cannot be "explained" in normal rational thought nor expressed through words. What it has to say and what it expresses is contained only and uniquely in it. This is true not necessarily of the thing it expresses.

This can be raised to the level of rational discourse. But it is then got at in a different way. Reason, in its middle ground, gets to its object by universalizing imagination. Art, on the lower fringe of reason, gets to its object by composing singular sensibles. Thus universal reason abstracts relation from imagination, but art gets to its object not by abstraction of form, but by imposition of form. It points the relation in the matter and therefore gets at its object through the positing.

In this, again, art resembles verbalization, which may be seen in this context as the putting of meaning into meaningless sounds. Language arises in this way as a social phenomenon when the arbitrary relation of significance is known and accepted by the group. But this is not necessary for the imposition of aesthetic relationality in art. To this extent, art is solitary and more like pure thought and contemplation, it is not a social activity, however much it may arise naturally and normally out of social activity. This character of the private comes to the fore when art reaches a high state of perfection, as in Beethoven, who late in his life no longer cared whether or not his works were appreciated—that they did something for him sufficed. In this he was like Aquinas, who at the end of his life could no longer bring himself to write. He could think profoundly, but he could not bring himself to express this thought. In one case, we have the purity of the aesthetic, in the other, the purity of the contemplative. Both are essentially solitary.

If this is so, then contemplation is not bound by what can be expressed in common language and what all or some or only a few can understand through communication in common language. Nor is art bound by the same strictures so that the artist must be able to explain his work, and give it public meaning.

This comparison suggests that the determination of how the symbol functions in the contemplative may indicate how it also functions in the aesthetic. I suppose here, that even the heights of contemplation never get away from the use of imagination. This means that I am not operating in a Neo-Platonic mode, in which contemplation is thought without imagination. I am operating in the Aristotelian mode, in which thought is never without imagination. We are men, not gods. We must be awake or at least sensing, and, through that, imagining, in order to be thinking. That is our human limitation and condition. This means that in such a condition, relation is always given as in such and such a content, but it is taken as in itself. This is the essence of abstraction. Thus, as given, it has the character of image and of the univocal and of representation. But, as taken, it has the character of the relational, it is not univocal and does not represent the singular content of the given. This relational character of the taken is expressed when we say, for example, not as in this or that, but as in itself. As in itself, it is image or representation of nothing. It simply is itself. Total identity has been reached.

Philosophers express this when they say that they are interested, for example, in motion, not as in this or that, but as in itself. The relationality, which is imaged in the *given* is that of "in"— a spatial relation. But the relationality which is in the *taken*, precisely not this, but *identity*. That we must express this as "in itself" indicates that we cannot, as the Neo-Platonists thought, rise to pure thought without reference to imagination, but rather that we can rise to pure thought and do and must through what we do with imagination. Imagination still remains "symbolic," but its symbolism becomes transcendent.

Let me suppose that this is always the purpose of reason—that it does not want to stay with the sensibly given immanent in sense experience, but get to the "beyond"—which I deliberately put in quotation marks to indicate that it really is not beyond, but is the sustaining whole, which is simply not seen as such in the initial experience, but is there and makes that experience possible by being there. It will then follow that, even in art, if we suppose that this works with sensible matter, but is a manifestation of reason, and aims at self-possession and God-possession—is thus radically theological—the endeavor to transcendentalize must manifest itself. It will then follow from this that the use of the sensible will not reduce the intellect to an "eye," but raise the eye to contemplation. What is symbolic in the aesthetic product must therefore be a means to this. And it must therefore work in some way akin to the way in which it works in human universal or scientific thought to achieve this transcendental result. As Aquinas puts it, it must work to bring the weakly intelligible to actual intelligibility.

But, in the light of what we have been considering, this can be put in a different way. We have been considering how reason, reaching down to imagination, can make imagination serve transcendental purposes. By parallel, we may be asking how reason can reach down to sensation—be in the eye and in the ear—and raise them to its transcendental purpose. How it can do this, if we can see this in any way, is how it transcendentalizes sensation. And that must be how symbol is in art.

Moreover, the analogy must be pressed, that reason, while passive for its first information from imagination—it gets the image from it and sees the intelligible in it, is nevertheless active in its further relation to imagination—it controls imagination for its own purposes. We speak of this commonly as concentration. In art, it must do the same for sensation—for the eye and the ear. As in the eye and the ear, it must make both transcend themselves. The eye must see more than a mere eye can, and the ear hear more than a mere ear can.

But there is again this difference that, whereas the intellect is passive with respect to the first intelligible and cannot choose what this will be, the artist is active and choosing from the beginning. Light will bend passing through a lens, and the intellect cannot choose that it shall not. Its only choice in this apprehension is the choice not to look. But the artist makes the nature by his choice. The things of his art are therefore like things of nature in that they come into being and can be sensed and understood. But they are not like things of nature in that they are what they are by his choice.

But, once he has made the choice, he becomes both passive and active. The aesthetic whole is not only him. Its effect upon him is like a mystical rapture. In this state, he has unexpected energy and seems to be driven rather than to work on his own. Every artist experiences this, often in the course of producing his work. Then everything goes well. Things begin to go badly when this being seized ceases to operate. The aesthetic whole no longer indicates clearly what next step to take. Or its ferocity simply exhausts the artist, and he must stop to recoup strength.

The impact of the whole is both cognitive and emotional, and this on the sense level and on the level of intellect and will. Thus Beethoven, in quartet 15, in the third movement couched in the Gregorian mode—the hymn of thanksgiving to God for the recovery of health—expresses first of all gratitude toward God for the recovery of health, and this in a slow movement—very slow—molto adagio. Then he expresses the joy of feeling health returning ("*neue Kraft fuhlend*"—"feeling new strength") with a more rapid movement—"andante". Then, as if to express shame for this feeling, he reverts to a slow movement—again "molto adagio" ("*mit innigster Empfindung*"—"with deepest feeling"). This feeling is therefore the combination of gratitude and joy, and thus looks both to God and self.

The structure of the movement thus reflects the alteration of psychology and the combination of feelings. These are therefore the root of the expression and, at the same time, the end. They thus originate the expression and are "got at" through it.   This indicates at least two poles in the aesthetic activity, and a mediating principle through which one is conjoined to the other. One pole is the subjective experience of sickness and recovery of health. The other pole is this same content objectified—the signified sickness and recovery of health. This is conjoined to the subjective pole through the medium which is the "making" of the musical composition. Through this making, the composer extrapolates or objectifies his otherwise purely subjective experience. In the light of our analysis, it is clear that he does this to get at it in another way or to possess it in experience. Through his art, he then comes to possess it as an experience in the form of objectification, which is peculiar to art.

It is important in understanding this to mention again the order of the intentional and of the real, and the order of making and doing. The intentional is immanent relationally within artists as knowers and willers which, insofar as it terminates in what is really distinct from them, makes that really distinct other term part of their being. Intentional activity thus begins and terminates in the agent. Making activity, on the contrary, begins in the agent, but terminates outside. To this extent, it is cut off from him. Thus, the tool is cut off in its being from the being of the craftsman, but, insofar as he knows it, forms part of his being. It is, in knowledge, the immanent term of the relationship—intention—which knowledge is. And this immanent term points relationally to another such really distinct term (which is therefore also intentionally possessed and part of the being of the knower as such), namely the effect which the tool is to produce, and, beyond that, the use of the effect by which the craftsman is to benefit.

Thus, doing embraces making such that it is the root of making, and making is an extension of it which points to another doing. Put more concretely, the craftsman, envisaging the use (a doing and specifically a possessing and an enjoyment), makes the tool to get at this. And, since the use which is thus the final purpose of the making is a benefit to himself, or, put more crudely but philosophically more lucidly, is himself benefitted, since use is possession of the benefitted self. When this conceptualization is extrapolated to infinity, use is enjoyment of or possession of the fully actualized self mediated through making. It is obvious what a world of possibilities lies in this understanding for illuminating the nature of society and, indeed, all other human phenomena. But our specific concern is with its use to illuminate the nature of artistic activity.

From the point of view of this use, and keeping the same example of the Beethoven of the fifteenth quartet, we can see that the beginning is Beethoven experiencing himself as recovering from illness and seeing this as an act of God's mercy for which he is duly grateful. The middle is the "making" of the music—the extrapolation or objectification of the subjective experience into the really distinct composition of sounds. The end is the final possession of himself as thus suffering and benefitted now, not only with the benefit of physical health, but with the benefit of possessing this *through art*, that is through making. Thus, what is first possessed as accepted or known to consciousness now becomes possessed as the "made" insofar as it is got at through making. So got at, it is filtered through the joy of the mind in perceiving beauty. And in this way, what otherwise is an experience at best tolerated is now an experience enjoyed and a possession of self which points ultimately to full possession of self, and, insofar as this points to knowledge and love of oneself who, as a creature, is "part" of God, possession of self as "part" of God and, to that extent, possession of God. Art thus manifests itself again, as does philosophy, it is at root the desire to possess God which draws the artist on. And it is the growing degree of such possession which constitutes artistic growth and the growing joy of the artist.

As this is manifested in the fifteenth quartet of Beethoven, the moods of the parts of the composition serve as the symbols of sickness and recovery of health and the expression of gratitude. These are therefore also "signs" or "symbols" of it. Thus, from the point of view of the total subjective experience, these form a natural psychological structure of psychological parts within a psychological whole. The aesthetic in the composition is its independence of this, such that, even if one did not grasp the psychological whole-part relationship, one would still grasp the aesthetic whole-part relationship. One would therefore enjoy the work even without knowing its relation to the psychological. But then the work would have no meaning, or, at least, not the meaning intended by the artist. In other words, as so many have said, it would *mean* nothing. It would *be*. We can take this to mean legitimately that the aesthetic can and indeed should be abstracted from symbolism and meaning as such in order to be appreciated in itself. But this is not the same as saying that ultimately it does not need the matrix of meaning for its ultimate sense, i.e., for why it is done at all.

These considerations seem to indicate that both conventional signs, such as words, and real signs, such as smoke, and the psychological consequences of various states of euphoria or depression may enter into works of art as symbols which, insofar as they do so enter, then point to the realities which society accepts them to represent. It also argues strongly that the finally signified, in either case, must not overwhelm the aesthetic whole-part relation, and, by doing this, destroy it. That has occurred often in the history of art, and is even an important consideration in critically judging this history. One could even go so far as to say that it is the crucial criterion for judging it.

This leads naturally to the next chapter, in which we shall consider the relationship between symbolism and the aesthetic and how they have concretely affected the history of art.

CHAPTER 8

Symbolism: The *Per Se* and the History of Art

If we understand the *per se* whole relation in the made, which, as such, is self-explanatory, and symbolism as essentially a pointing to the beyond, in other words as that which takes its meaning from something outside of it, then the "history" of art becomes intelligible. It is not a linear movement toward a terminal goal—the self-possession which we have posited, but a cyclical movement between the predominance of the *per se* marked by moments of equilibrium in individual artists in which both forces have been in balance. This has been the case, it would seem, not in "schools" of artists so much as in individual artists. And this would seem to indicate that artistic activity, although needing generally some sort of matrix—a school or social conditions or some such factors—reaches equilibrium only in individuals. Groupings of individuals seem, in fact, not only to impede creativity, but also to impede this equilibrium.

In the equilibrium, it is obvious that the symbolic or something equivalent to it must originally prevail. This is because the aesthetic, as we have theorized upon it, is essentially mediate to the symbolized in the aesthetic. Insofar as this is true, it takes its sense from the symbolized and therefore also its teleology. One is inclined to produce the aesthetic only to get to the symbolized.

But the medium as such is distinct from the end, and therefore can be abstracted from it. In the development of art, this is what seems first to occur in decoration. Or, perhaps, it might be more accurate to say that decoration is first brought to being within the context of symbolism or practical use, and then is separated from the latter so as to stand alone. Then symbolism is added. Thus, practical use and relation to the practical end—with religious overtness and perhaps magical in the practical tool—comes first. Within this as a matrix, decoration then develops. The decoration is separated out from the matrix by a sort of abstraction. The abstraction is then reversed when reference or relation to the extrinsic is added as "meaning" through symbolism.

At this point, a tension arises. The reference to the extrinsic tends to take over and determine the parts of the "aesthetic whole" so that they are not such at all. This occurs, for example, in a period of "realism," as in Greco-Roman art or nineteenth century academic art in France and Germany. Such periods are then most likely to be followed by periods in which external reference and therefore symbolism is totally rejected and the aesthetic is proposed in its pure abstraction as self-sufficient and in no need of the meaning reference, as in twentieth century Abstractionist art. During the cyclical movement, genius asserts itself always when some artists meld the two, just as Rembrandt did, or Rouault, or Van Gogh.

The tension which such artists manage to resolve is thus not that of subjectivity and objectivity, as is often said, especially in comparing western art with eastern, but that of the purely decorative and that of the "meaningful." Or better, of that art in which the reference of meaning dominates the aesthetic and dictates its parts so that they are not truly parts of the aesthetic, but parts of "representation" alone, and that art which deliberately cuts itself off from all reference to what is beyond the aesthetic, that is to all meaning.

Those who stress the nature orientation of eastern art and therefore its objectivity, and playing down of subjectivity, are not taking into account the full phenomenon of artistic activity. In this, the artist begins with nature or the model, to which he then reacts subjectively. He then objectivizes this subjective reaction in the aesthetic medium and through this gets to a possession of the self, that is to say, of the subjective.

In this, oriental art is not different from western art, and individualism is necessarily involved in both. This latter tends to disappear only in art which arises in a magical, religious (a sacramental) context which dictates form, as in Egyptian art as opposed to Greek. Such art emerges within the context of representing the magical action which must not be altered, since its own uniqueness and not human choice has efficacy. The greatness and truth of the aesthetic in this is the ability of the artist to determine the parts so as to make them truly aesthetic—as if independent of the dictated form—and yet represent it. It is so in the art of Egypt and much oriental art. And it is so also in the medieval art of Christendom, which Coomaraswamy considers akin to oriental and therefore intelligible to the oriental mind. This is because medieval art also begins with the meaning and moves to the aesthetic, rather than with the purely decorative, from which one moves out to meaning. The crucial differentiating principle is thus not subjectivity (with possible individualism) and objectivity, but illegitimate dominance of meaning and total severance from meaning; or dominance of symbolism (illegitimate, that is) and total severance from any symbolism.

The fact that this occurs poses a question for the history of art which is similar to questions posed for the history of philosophy and morality. Thus, as Aristotle remarks, all science and all philosophy is gained and then lost over the period of time; but the myth perdures. I abstract for the moment from the question which the history of science poses!

Let us suppose that all of oriental and western art are theological in their term, as I have already argued. Why, then, do they undergo cyclical alterations rather than move linearly toward their terms and at an equal pace? Undergoing such cyclical alterations, they both move toward their true term, and, at alternating times, away from it.

Something akin to this occurs also in the moral sphere, where societies rise in a "golden age," but then eventually fall away from its purity, and finally collapse to be succeeded by others. So, also in art, the cyclical movement seems to be one which rises to a period during which the aesthetic goes beyond mere decoration or its equivalent—the abstraction of the aesthetic in itself—to the melding of the aesthetic and meaning, and then falls into decay with the domination or destruction of the aesthetic by the meaning—in what is often called "realism." In opposition to this the movement toward the abstracted aesthetic devoid of meaning arises again as in modern Abstractionism.

Some indication of why such cycles occur may be found in what clearly occurs in the social cycle. It reaches its peak in the golden age—the "Garden of Eden stage"—when the majority of its members best obey the traditions through which alone they can survive and which they have learned by a long social induction. When they begin to lose confidence in these, then society goes into decline. And not even the finest spirits can prevent this, as is evident in the decline and fall of both Rome and Greece. Such fine minds cannot persuade the masses to seek again in their daily actions the goal which their society once so well sought. This goal, therefore, no longer draws them. The true good is inoperative, and therefore the value which it ultimately gives to the intermediate actions falls also away. It also no longer attracts as it naturally should. A traditional explanation of this phenomenon in the moral order is that, while a human being is necessarily drawn to the true human goal of happiness in general, he errs concerning its concrete embodiment. So erring, he chooses, as if it were ultimate happiness, what is in fact only a means to this. This is what causes the moral decay.

Artistic decay, if we parallel it to this, would result from the same phenomenon. The true goal of artistic activity is erroneously identified with the artistic means to this. Artists then make the means their "god." It thus loses its character of means in this false conception and becomes apparently the terminal end. This could occur either through the identification of the aesthetic in itself without reference to meaning as the apparent end, or the aesthetic with a truly mediate terminal meaning.

If such an end is factually achieved, then it is clearly experienced as mediate; as unsatisfactory because the true end is not a matter of choice, but of necessity. And this being so, the intermediate, even if it seems when not achieved to be ultimate, must reveal itself once achieved to be unsatisfactory. The artist, having experienced this, just as the moral person, must then look for another content which will be truly satisfying. He thus divides and multiplies the apparent ultimate end such that the approach to the true end is unifying, whereas the approach to what is only apparently the end is fragmenting. This approach is therefore toward alienation from self-possession, whereas the true approach is toward self-possession. In more contemporary terms, the true approach is integrative, whereas the false or apparent dissolves the unity of the end.

This being so, it is clear that an approach to the apparent end on the moral or philosophical level can hardly be reconciled with an approach to the true end on the aesthetic. One cannot really posit God possessed through the possession of self as the end of the artistic and deny this as the end of the moral and the philosophic. To do so is to deprive the capacity for action of the very principle of action. If self-possession is that principle, and if its truth and value are denied in philosophy and morals, respectively, then its availability for artistic activity is eliminated.

That is why ancient Greek thought saw a correlation between virtue and philosophical insight, and, one could say, insight into the aesthetic. In principle, these, as coming from the same source, must so relate to one another that they depend upon and reinforce one another. They divide, in fact, as we have said, the qualities of the terminal experience of self-possession. The true philosophy of the history of human activity therefore shows it to be linear.

From this point of view, then, the *de facto* history of philosophy, morals, and art is the history of the movement toward a false or apparent terminal end. Necessarily, therefore, it is cylindrical. This is because the apparent end *seems* to contain the true end, and therefore, even through it, the true end always operates, and this naturally. But, insofar as the apparent end is false, the movement always necessarily peaks and then declines. And thus philosophy, morals, society, civilization, and art move always cyclically.

The history of culture carries always the remembrance of this in the "mythical" quantification of the times of the cycles. Thus, they are for Plato and those from whom he draws the number periods of 10,000 years, and, for the Etruscans, the *per omnia saecula saeculorum,* through all the age of ages, which entered into Christian liturgy. In essence, these really say that there is no ultimate end toward which art, philosophy, and morals *de facto* move linearly, but one toward which they move and from which they recede. To say this is to say that life has factually no ultimate meaning, nor art, nor philosophy. The Greek myth of Sisyphus clearly embodies this conviction. It is a myth grounded on human experience, and, so far as it goes, antithetical to the simpler conviction of the linear movement to the "happy hunting grounds" or the Christian salvation conviction of the eschatological coming of the "kingdom."

If this is so, then it is clear that art, just as philosophy and morals, cannot separate itself from concrete human action. And, if in the moral sphere, from the Christian point of view, this is reducible to "original sin," which causes the cycling, so it is reducible to something similar, if not the same, in art and philosophy.

In philosophy, one could assert that Existentialism is precisely the response to this. There must therefore also be a parallel in art. This is the same as to ask the question: what in art corresponds to the salvation from original sin in morals, and the Existentialist approach in philosophy? The question, put in this form, associates the two approaches closely. And this makes one think of James Joyce's obvious parallel of salvation which functions as a sign effecting what it signifies. By this it "saves," or removes the principle of cycling so that one can again approach directly to the true terminal point of all human action. Thus, action again becomes linear and therefore eschatological. It has a "happy hunting ground" and a "kingdom of God." It is freed from the eternal return of the ancient myths and the continual transmigration of souls and the *saecula saeculorum* of the Etruscans.

CHAPTER 9

The Intentionality of Art: Relation as the Fundamental Analytical Tool

From all of the preceding considerations, it is clear that relation is the fundamental category, whether of reality or of the mind, for the analysis and understanding of art. For, if this is the term of artistic activity, then the artist is related to it. As artist, he "holds himself toward it." And, if his subjective state, as we have exemplified this is the case of Beethoven, relates to him, then that subjective state also "holds itself to" the aesthetic term. And, if that term is a whole made of up of parts, then those parts "hold themselves toward" the whole. And, if the whole plus the parts symbolize something beyond—the "meant," then they "hold themselves toward it." And, if the "meant beyond" is truly ultimately the self as possessed, then in art the self, as potentially self-possessing, holds itself through mediating factors toward the self as actually possessed—ultimately, as actually totally possessed.

So understood, art is then a relationship strung out between the partially self-possessing artist and the totally self-possessing artist. This is the term not only of art, as we have already stressed, but also of morality and speculation, which are therefore also distinct relationalities to the common term. And, if that common term is the grasp of oneself as one truly is, namely as not God but to God, then the ultimate term of all of these relations is God, they are in truth theological. And the being of the person is that of one who is not God, but grasps this in its truth and loves it in its truth and rests in it in its truth. In this way, one can come to understand the human person—reversing the relational structure—as "thrown out" from God, and then as moving back to God, while ultimately still standing off from him.

The situation so described is thus a thoroughgoing relational structure. This being so, I want now to introduce one preliminary notion of a form or possibility of relation which is crucial to the understanding of its use in this analysis. This is the notion of a relation which is unified, or one, at one of its terms and multiplied or many at the other. Such a relation takes the symbolical form of a "fan" rather than the usual one of the arrow. Figure 9-1 shows the difference between how we are accustomed to think of the relational structure, as unitary at both terms, and then how we are asked to think of it here as a unitary term related to many.

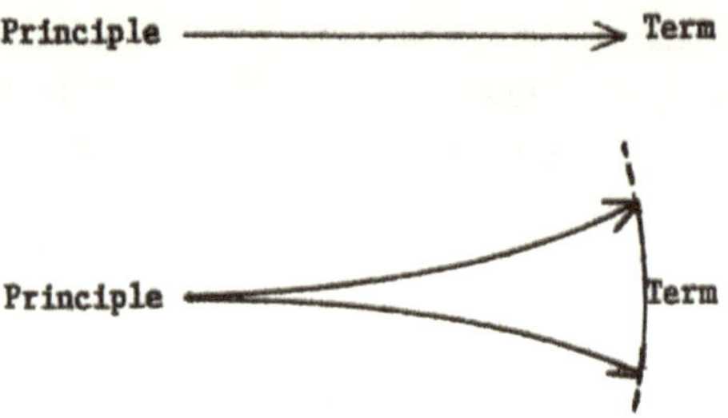

Figure 9-1

Saint Thomas Aquinas uses it to conceptualize creation. Creation is, for him, simply a relation or the relation of all creatures to God such that they are multiple, but their termination in God in one. This is so not only at one instant in time when the multiplicity of the *not God* all terminates in the simplicity—read identity or unity—of God but it is also true in all time—in past, present, and future, which may extend, as far as the possibilities of reality go and as far as reason can conclude, into infinity in either direction or in both directions. The actualization of either possibility depends, for him, not on the "natures" of created things, but upon the choice of God. Choice, therefore, for him, is the paradigm of creation, not geometrical reasoning.

Of course, *for man*, reasoning is the only accessible paradigm. And that is his essential limitation in understanding being. Descartes made this clear to modern man, although he did not make clear its essentially anthropological character as opposed to the theological character of religious revelation—the viewpoint from the side of God. Being, for modern man, has been being as it *seems* to man rather than being as it is for God. This latter is accessible to us only through revelation of his choice, not through knowledge of the nature of things. Thus, modern man, insofar as he departs from this view, sees God and creation through the paradigm of nature—therefore God as the *imago hominis* or the *imago naturae*—whereas that tradition, which exists even in modern times and in modern man which sees man as the *imago Dei* basically through divine choice.

This was the fourth philosophy of Schelling which so deeply influenced Kierkegaard, and it is the fundamental philosophy of modern and contemporary Existentialism. To this extent, both rejoin the basic intuition of Aquinas, who sees the limitation of science and philosophy in its need to explain what is through nature and the necessity of nature, whereas its real explanation is divine choice, which neither nature nor the necessity of nature control.

However this may be, the application of the fan form of the symbol of relation to the complex structure or the aesthetic is of considerable interest and, speculatively, highly suggestive. It suggests first of all that the self—artistic "ego"—holds itself as the unified term of a relation—an intentionality—which terminates in the multiplicity of the aesthetic parts which are themselves the fan term of a relation to the unity of the aesthetic whole. Thus, the aesthetic whole stands over against the self as a unified term, similar in this to the self, but connecting to the self through the fan term, which is the interconnection of the aesthetic parts.

The aesthetic parts then connect directly to the meant parts of the meant whole as symbols to symbolized, and the meant parts to the meant whole as to the unified term of the relation which structures the meaningful whole. Through this interconnection, the aesthetic whole and the meant whole are thus relationally connected, and this connection ultimately connects with self-possession and, through that, with God-possession. If this is so, it means, of course, that artistic production, in its full relationallity, aims at God-possession, but it does not mean that it can produce of itself such possession. It may mean, at least, only that its nature is to aim in this direction and always to tend in this direction, but never, of itself, to be able to seize upon the term. This is the same as to say that no act of aesthetic productivity, just as no act of speculation or morality, has the capacity actually to seize upon self-possession or upon God-possession, but that all are means to this end. As such, they define the nature of man and determine the nature of his operations. They therefore make him a being of the in-between, not a being of the end—actually, that is, although potentially he is a being of the end.

A more complete relational schema of the larger situation would then be in Figure 9-2.

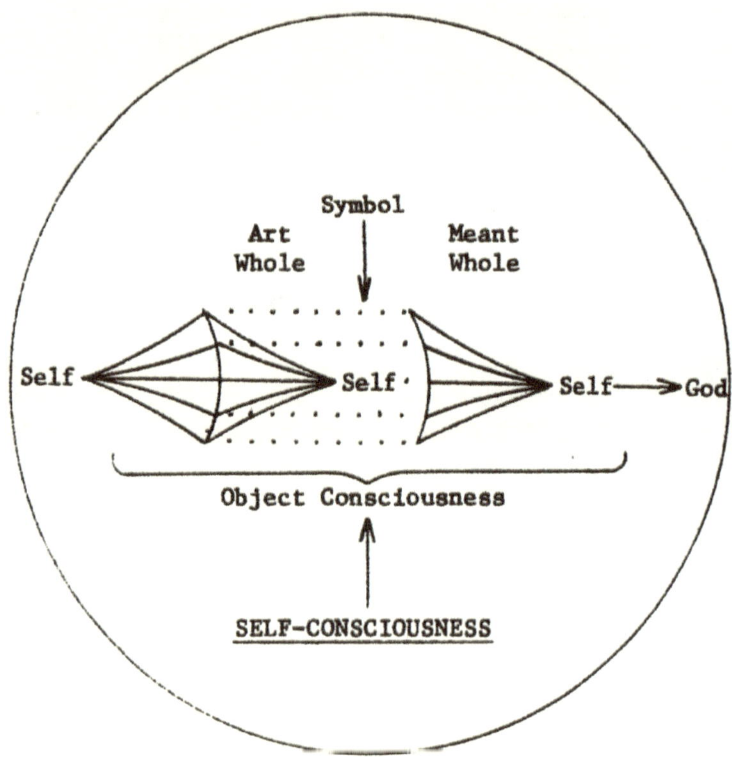

Figure 9-2

In the interpretation of this schema of relations, the relation to the object, or to the non-ego or to the not-self, is real and primary and constitutive of the nature of the object knowledge. This means that it is not to be interpreted as a relation of similarity or represent-ation following upon the presence in the mind of a similitude of objective reality—the representative theory which is commonly assumed to be classical and avowedly is modern—but rather as a real relation to the object which itself is part of the intentional being of the knowing subject, such that, through it, both itself and the object are part of its being. In this sense, the knower is the object.

Therefore this classical theory is known as that of "identification," such that Aristotle can say of the act of knowing that in it the knower and the known are the same. This being so, through knowing, the knower becomes really what is ontologically diverse, while the ontological diversity still holds. Aristotle axiomatized this understanding in the definition of knowing as the becoming of the other insofar as it still remains other. And Aquinas characterized intellectual knowing, as Heidegger correctly observed in the beginning of *Sein und Zeit* as that whereby we become all things—*quo omnis fieri*. The causative principle to which he attributes this becoming immediately—the so-called "active intellect," which he argues each human person individually has—he then characterizes as a principle by which we make ourselves all other things—*quo omnia facere*. Knowing is therefore a real relation of similitude, which begins and ends in the knower, constitutes the entity of the knowing of the knower, and thereby brings about that what is not the knower outside of knowledge is, as term of the real relation, really the knower in knowledge.

But what this real relationship of object-consciousness does for the knower with respect to the really diverse is carried further in self-consciousness. In this, no relationship of similarity intervenes. And no relationality at all is constitutive of the knowing. Pure and simple identification functions here. The knower is *in the knower*. In the case of the Divine Knower, Aristotle can then axiomatize the situation in the famous statement—much beloved of Hegel and often quoted by him—that the "object" of intellection is intellection itself.

In the human knower, this is not the case, nor is self-consciousness primary. The human knower is therefore held to be self-conscious through reflection upon his primarily objective knowledge. The human knower comes to self-knowledge through object knowledge. This is true even for knowledge of other persons. That is also knowledge of the other, qua other, through which, then, self-knowledge is mediated. But, of course, the "other" in this case is not simply an object in the sense in which other things of nature are. Yet it is still true that the other person truly is other and yet, through knowledge, part of the being of the knower. But that relationally terminal part of the being of the knower is itself a knower. And one therefore does not, or should not, use that other. But this consideration is not germane to our present purposes, nor is it fitting here to stop and develop in its entirety a theory of human knowledge or volition or causation (which is reducible ultimately to the conjunction of both), but, rather, presupposing them, and holding the given schema as representative of them, to interpret what we have already said in its light.

In Chapter 2, we dealt with the nature of the philosophy of art and there stated that it is a critical, reflex look at all that is involved in artistic activity. In accordance with the particular philosophical tradition which this critique follows, that activity aims ultimately at self-possession—or the terminal realization of the full human potential, which is had in terminal interiority whereby the self grasps itself to the full extent of its intelligibility, loves itself in this grasp, and in the grasp and love has aesthetic rest. We indicated that this full turning into self sees the self for what it is, that is to say, not God, but dependent upon him by a relation of dependency, which relation it then also grasps to the full extent of the human capacity. This is to say that it "takes possession of God" in this sense, to whom it essentially relates and from whom it stands off by this relation. And, since the soul thus loves itself as it is, it loves itself *not to be God* and it loves God as the "whole" of which it is a "part."

The Figure 9-2 indicates, then, that the relationship of artistic activity, or the series of relations involved in it, thrust through to the terminal point, which is God. From the point of view of this analysis, it does not matter whether or not a particular artist is convinced of this any more than it matters whether or not someone involved in moral action realizes that the sense of such action is God or that someone involved in scientific and philosophical pursuits realizes the same. Regardless of this, all action here and now is no more than a means to the specified end. And that end is not a matter of choice, although the means through which one moves toward it are. Thus, the tradition states the situation in this way: the good *in communi* (as a universal) is set by nature; but the good *in concreto* (that which seems to be the ultimately satisfying good to the individual) is a matter of choice. That the particular choice was not correct is seen by the individual when, if he manages to achieve it, it leaves him unsatisfied. This is because the true good is not really a matter of individual choice, but only the means to it, and, when what is only the terminal good according to appearance is actually achieved, this then becomes clear. It does not, in fact, satisfy.

The circles in Figure 9-2 indicate this by symbolically presenting the reaches of consciousness. These are not to be taken solely as waves, and thus sequential and moving out toward the possession of the self and of God, but in the inverse direction too. In that inverse and teleological direction, it is, therefore, the possession of self and of God which is pulling the soul (or, by another and equally familiar metaphor attracting the soul). Thus the self thrusts toward God and God draws it to do this. In these reverse actions, the latter is prior. The soul is what it is and does what it does because God draws it to self-possession and possession of himself. Drawing it to this, he gives it that sort of nature which can move toward this goal and eventually reach it.

In the movement, insofar as it is experienced as seeking to take possession, the artist is most strongly aware of his initial stance. This leads immediately to a making with sensible matter (as opposed to or distinguished from the doing which characterizes the moral movement or the speculative). The movement to the making from the original stance is thus often characterized quite naturally by the artist as a "seeking to express" oneself. The artists speaks of wanting to "get out" something which is within, as if the end of the action were already immanent and its sole purpose were to communicate that fact. Communication seems, in this consciousness of what artistic activity is, prime.

But, as we noted in Chapter 3, speaking of the genesis of artistic activity, the original working with sensible parts leads to the discovery and choice of the aesthetic whole in the concrete. Then that takes over and the artist feels pulled rather than self-moving. This feeling of being drawn gives artistic activity the character of the ecstatic, as if the drawing were so violent as to take artists outside of themselves. This makes artistic activity often seem a frenzy, and inspiration rather than self-expression then seems to characterize it. The artists feels as if there were another force, much more powerful than the self or the origin, which is within the activity itself, and in it expresses itself or moves the artist to whatever it is that he does.

Figure 9-2 therefore breaks this down immediately to the fan relation of the self to the aesthetic parts and, through them, to the aesthetic whole. By the broken lines which tie this structure to the meant whole, it then indicates that the aesthetic parts relate directly to the meant parts of a significant whole. Those meant parts relate, by a similar fan relation, to the meant whole. Thus, through this tissue of relations, the aesthetic whole itself relates to meaning, and this is necessarily through symbolism, which is, in fact, defined as to its meaning in this context. And that meaning is identified as such, as "significance."

Figure 9-2 then indicates that the meant whole necessarily points to the meant self, and that to God. The entire process, by this fact, becomes theological. Thus, diagramatically, the beautiful (the aesthetic) and the true (the meant and the intelligible) and the good (ultimately the attracting self and God) all tie relationally together. And the process of artistic production is one in which, whether consciously or not, these elements distinguish themselves out. Thus, art becomes to this extent critical, as philosophy is. That is to say, art comes to realize all of the factors at play in its activity in their unity and distinction.

Later on, in dealing with James Joyce and his convictions concerning the situation, we will see in what peculiar way he equates the symbolic aspect of this diagrammed relational whole of aesthetic activity with the sacramental, that is how he conceives of the symbolic element as making what it signifies, as thereby producing aesthetic salvation from "sin," and thus becoming a substitute theology, as it were. Now my concern is to situate aesthetic activity in the full range of reason.

CHAPTER 10

The Specific Intentionality of Art:
Symbol in Reason as a Whole and in Art as a Part
of the Whole

The analysis of the preceding chapter endeavors to expose, at least, some of the relational structures in aesthetic activity. At this point in our investigation, it is not necessary to enter into greater detail. But it is necessary to situate the aesthetic analysis in the broader analysis of reason as a whole and of human activity as a whole.

As shown in Figure 10-1, from that broader point of view, one could either take the self as a unit point of departure from which the moral, the speculative, and the aesthetic fan out relationally, or one could take these three avenues of human expression as themselves the fan end of a relation which is unitary. In either case, one takes the side of the "being drawn" or of the "actively moving self toward."

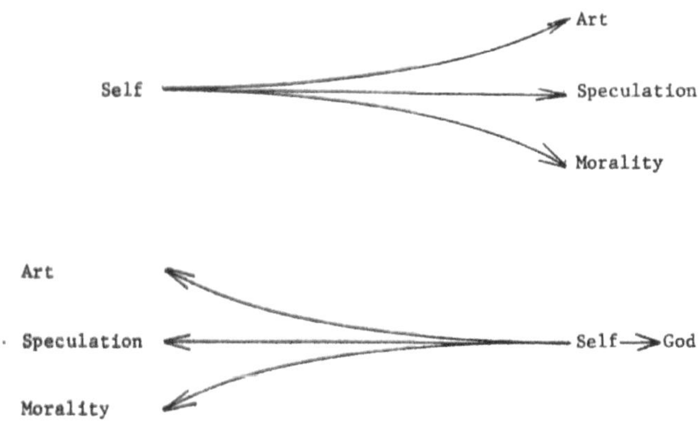

Figure 10-1

In the former case, one stresses the unity of the initial self and the trifurcation of the developing self. In the latter case, one stresses the trifurcation of the initial self and the movement outward unity of the developing self. In this latter case, the developing self seeks integration and, eventually, self-possession, that is not merely correlation of the different, but identity of the apparently or intermediately differentiated.

In either case, the initial self is thinking—specifically reasoning, and willing. In our present consideration, we abstract from the volitional and concentrate upon the rational. This itself has a range such that there is a highest and a lowest use of reason, or a use of reason which is closest to pure intelligence and one which approximates, within the range of reason, to the sensible.

But there is also a range of being beyond the rational and a range of being below the rational. This gives rise to the terminology: "supra-rational" and "infra-rational." These are not at all the same thing as the "irrational." They do not, in other words, contradict reason, but they lie off the edge of its normal use and must be got to, if at all, in a fringe-type use of metaphor. Let us add to this that, throughout the entire range and into both the supra- and infra-rational, the symbolic has a role to play and, indeed, a role which characterizes human reason.

We have studied that role, through the diagram, in its specifically aesthetic function. To complete this, we must now study it in its full range. In that full range, symbol functions *always.* One can take this to be what Aristotle meant when he asserted, contrary to Plato and all Platonists, that there is nothing in reason which does not get into it through imagination, or that what is actually in reason is potentially in imagination. Imagination, in this theory, is the potential symbol of reason, and actual reason is imaginative symbol rationalized.

This might seem to limit the range of reason by excluding from it what cannot be a content of imagination. But that is to misunderstand the richness of imagination and its function as a symbol. This must be true if it is true that by reason the human knower can become all things, but, at the same time, only with the aid of imagination. This says that imagination is all things—as broad as reason, therefore, but always only potentially and within the context of the use of imagination by reason.

Thus, the human knowing principle composes sense and intelligence. For this reason, it has a range. It extends all the way from the lowest external sense to highest operation of intellect. As a consequence, there are operations of the intellectual principle which come closest to sense, and immediately to imagination, and operations which are furthest from sense and imagination. These latter, although they are the furthest, are not so in the sense that they escape the interconnection. If they could, then it would not be true that intellection contains nothing but what is first in sense. Besides such contents there would then be others, as in the Platonic theory of knowledge, which are in no way in sense. Human intellect would then have insights which totally transcend sense, and a mode of operation which transcends reason. In the theory of human knowledge which is here operative, we are supposing that this is not so.

As I have elsewhere argued, this leads to the conviction that the principle of interconnection between reason and sense is relation. Sense knowledge presents the terms of relation and rational knowledge actually unites them or actually perceives their true ontological union.

Supposing this to be so, then one can characterize the range of reason, including its fringes, in this way. The lowest fringe is the perception by reason of relations which are of such a sort that they cannot be abstracted from their sensible matrices. These, I will argue, are the relations of part to whole in the aesthetic product. Other relations are such that they can be abstracted and thus seen in themselves. Others again are such that they form a part of wholes—infinite wholes—and therefore, although pointing to such wholes, are never adequate to them. And through them, therefore, one cannot get to the whole as it is in itself directly. This is the upper fringe of rational operation.

Both in upper fringe and in the lower fringe, the situation is such that the intelligible content for reason cannot be abstracted and seen in itself directly, but must be got at indirectly, that is, through a medium. The medium is thus metaphor, symbol, or sign.

That is to say, it is something other than the intelligible content in itself, which other *points to* this content.

Thus, where abstraction is possible, then the relational intelligibility can be confronted directly in itself. Where abstraction is not possible, then the intelligibility, which is got at through relation, cannot be directly confronted. It must then be indirectly confronted through symbol. This means that it is confronted through a likeness or similarity or "representation"—all of which signify insight into what the thing is. What the thing "is," is thus seen through something similar to it, not by its being in itself. What it is in its own right is thus hidden from direct confrontation.

This is either because the intelligibility of the thing in itself is too weak for us, or too strong in itself. In the former case, it is invisible to the human eye—although not unseen by the divine, and in the latter, it overpowers the human eye. The human eye can look at the galaxies in the evening sky, but see nothing. But it cannot look at the noonday sun without damage. In both cases, a medium must intervene. The eye looks through the telescope or at a photograph. The eye looks at the illuminated grass. The intellect sees the meant content through the whole-part aesthetic product whose relational structure it cannot abstract from its sensible matrix. The intellect sees the trans-rational through parables, symbolism, metaphor, and analogy.

In the former case, the intellect gets at what is accessible in no other way or what is accessible in another way, but what is pleasing in a special way when got at through the aesthetic. In this case, the intellect uses symbols not because of necessity, but because of choice. In the case of that which transcends the rational, the intellect has no choice. It cannot get at this in any other way. And in both, negation predominates.

This is true, of course, even in abstraction. There, the intellect speaks of its intelligible content as being understood not as in this or that, but as in itself. So we commonly identify the philosopher as distinct from the scientist as the one who speaks of motion not as in this or that subject, but as in itself. Some think that this use of the relationship of in, which is obviously spatial in origin, as unjustified and as therefore making "philosophical" discourse "mystical" or meaningless. Others argue that not only is this not so, but it is an even more profound truth that the denial of the possibility of this use of the relationship of "in-ness" is the denial of the possibility of scientific discourse entirely and, even ordinary discourse. From this latter point of view, toward which more recent linguistic analysts tend and, among the scientists, for many years Werner Heisenberg—to mention only one—such a use of "in" is not only self-validating, but meaning-giving to all discourse.

Supposing this to be so, we can then distinguish the aesthetic, properly so-called, from the scientifically rational (mathematics, science, and philosophy, as well as ordinary practical knowledge) at least in this that the relationality of the aesthetic cannot be abstracted from the sensible matrix in this way. For the aesthetic, there is no such thing as the *Pietā* in itself or the *Last Supper* in itself. Nor is it proper to speak of either work as the concretization of a universal. For the same reason, it is not possible to teach someone "why" these are great masterpieces of art. Nor can one discourse, in abstraction, about what makes them beautiful. To the extent that all discourse is abstractive, one cannot therefore discourse about them at all. One can only point.

Thus, with respect to the purely aesthetic, the negative does not function at all. One cannot say of it—"not as in this or that, but as *in itself*." To speak of the *Pietā* not as in the Carrara marble in which it was carved or in any other material, but as in itself, is therefore to speak nonsense. What Logical Positivism has argued against traditional metaphysics is thus vindicated for fallacious art criticism. It speaks nonsense. Recognizing this, artists have traditionally been opposed to critics. They see them as those who cannot paint or draw and therefore write about painting or drawing without being able to put themselves really into the situation of the artist. The critics lay down abstract norms and judge artistic production according to them, whereas the artist denies even the existence of such norms and makes his own purpose to be the only norm and asks to be judged by that. There is something to be said for both sides, but that fact points at least to the peculiar intentionality of the aesthetic. Its relationality cannot be abstracted from its sensible matrix. So, whatever one has to say about it in abstract discourse cannot touch upon this. Of this one can only say— "it is good" or "it is a masterpiece" or "I like it." But one can never say, in terms of abstract form, why it is good or why it is extremely good or why one likes it. From the point of view of the viewer, artistic judgments are witness to subjective experience, not abstract grounding.

This does not make the object of the aesthetic purely subjective nor irrational, but simply non-abstractive. As non-abstractive, as inextricably embedded in the sensible matrix, it therefore, cannot, properly speaking, be taught. That is what I take Aristotle to be saying, when he attributes the making of metaphors to "inspiration" or "genius." Teaching takes place through the universal and therefore through abstraction. But the aesthetic as such cannot be abstracted. Therefore, it cannot be taught. And yet it is there, and recognized to be there with certainty!

The aesthetic is as objective, therefore, as objective science, but its objectivity is specific, or put in other terms, its intentionality is specific. Because of this, one can only say of it that, when it is seen, it is seen. And this fact is manifested subjectively and psychologically by the quality of the seeing—it pleases. It is not in this, that the seeing makes the pleasant and that the beautiful is thus purely subjective, but rather that the seeing of the objectively beautiful causes a subjective reaction which is peculiar to the aesthetic, namely that of satisfaction, of rest, or of pleasure.

For traditional thought, these are all the same seen from different points of view. From one point of view, seeing the beautiful satisfies, and, one wants no more. From another point of view, this is to come to rest. And from the traditional philosophy, the essence of pleasure is the fulfillment of a capacity—at least the relative fulfillment. It comes to rest in its object.

From the point of view of the relational analysis, then, one can establish a range. In this range, the absolute point of departure can be taken, again symbolically, as the non-related term given in sensation, thus as terms without relations. Next to these there are then terms with relations, but not abstractable from the sensible matrix. Next to these there are, then, terms with relations but capable of being abstracted. At the very fringe of reason there is then the non-relational self-contained which has, in itself, all the richness of relational being, but without relationality. This is shown schematically in Figure 10-2.

In range 1, at the very fringe of reason, the non-relational self-contained term has, in itself, all of the richness of the relational. Reason can see the relation embedded in sensibility, but it cannot generalize it.

In range 2, reason can generalize through abstraction—using negation. For example, in this way, it comes to speak of motion, not as in this or that subject but, as in itself. This is to relate motion to motion or to say "motion in motion." And by such constructions, all abstract thought proceeds! And from such thought it can, in certain cases, then concretize, as it does when it makes a *tool*. Of this, it knows both what the tool is supposed to do and this concrete exemplification of it. In other words, what it is in itself, and therefore, how this exemplifies that. Consequently, in this use of reason, teaching is possible. One presents the abstract to the student, and then one proceeds to its application in the concrete.

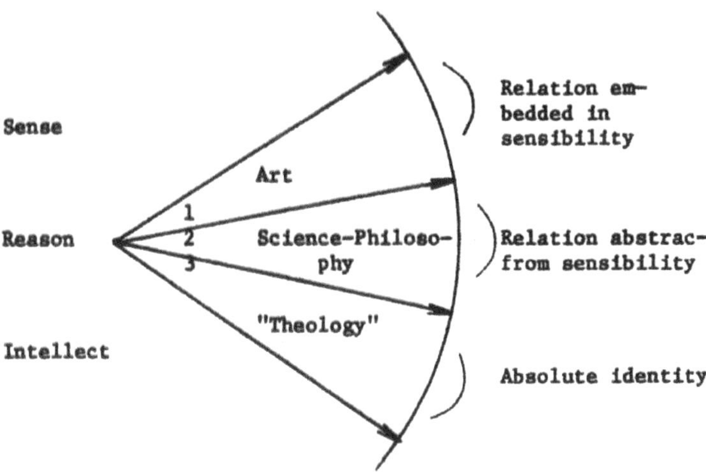

Figure 10-2

In range 3, the positive is minimal and the negative maximal. There, reason ignores more than it knows. Thus, it knows that God loves, but it does not know specifically what this means. It asserts this by saying that God loves, but not as a human being loves.

Thus, in range 1, reason uses symbols through defect of intelligibility. In range 3, it uses symbols because the intelligibility is excessive—"To what shall I compare the kingdom of heaven. It is like a mustard seen." This parable says, in effect, that all of the richness of the mustard seed is contained within the richness of being of the "kingdom of heaven" or of salvation—and infinitely more. This is not the case in range 2. The fullness of the richness of essential humanity is contained in each human person.

CHAPTER 11

The Anchoring of the Aesthetic in the Mathematical

The study of the history of art and of artistic products shows that there is a close relationship between the aesthetic and the mathematical. The aesthetic even seems sometimes to grow out of the mathematical. So, for example, Celtic ornamentation, if carefully analyzed, often shows, if it does not always show, an apparently mathematical point of departure. The artist seems to have begun with the rule and the compass, and then to have moved off from them. This is well-known for the architecture of classical times, which begins in many cases in clearly determinable mathematical relations and then stays often close to them, as in the laying out of proportions for Greek temples or for Greek urns. Jay Hambridge called attention to this in his works on "dynamic symmetry."

Of course, in these two examples, there is the difference that the architect does not move away from specified mathematical relations, but stays with them, whereas the Celtic artist, and artists in general, do move away. For them, the mathematical point of departure, if this is in fact taken, is not something to stay with because of the necessities of stresses and strains in structure, but something to start from as suggestive. Mathematics in this use is a jumping off point rather than an intrinsic and rigid determinant of the finished work of art.

This kinship is also witnessed to in the way in which a mathematician speaks of his reasonings. There is no other field of rational science where the adept is nearly naturally inclined to describe the reasonings in aesthetic or nearly aesthetic terms. Two proofs will be compared for their elegance and beauty. Simplicity combined with accuracy often draws this characterization. This is similar to the reaction of the artist who seeks to obtain an aesthetic result with the fewest means possible. Not that the fewness of the parts is what essentially constitutes the simplicity, but that the fewness of the parts combined with the obtaining of the same effect does.

So the later Rembrandt held that the fewer the strokes necessary to achieve the same result, the better. In a sense, this is to give the work of art the property of integrity. It has all those parts and only those parts which it needs.

Simplicity, in a kindred sense, is found in scientific theory. That theory which, with many others, equally well explains data (in the sense in which this is done by empirical theory), but which is the simplest, is the one to be chosen. Both the ancients and the moderns who agree on this, did not think that this had ontological significance, but only logical. What is simplest for human understanding is not necessarily the truth of reality.

But beyond this understanding and pursuit of the simple in scientific theory—which has some of the ramifications of the aesthetic, but not all (who is to say that the geometrical complexities of the Ptolemaic theory area not more beautiful than the geometry of the Copernican or the Keplerian)—there is also a genuine impinging of the aesthetic upon scientific theory in its mathematical physical aspect, that is in its quantitative rather than is qualitative aspect. This is the carry over into physics of the aspect of the beautiful through its presence in mathematics. The consequence is that theoretical physicists today are beginning to take seriously the factor of the aesthetic in scientific theory. They thus ask themselves: what would make the data or the theory more beautiful? And, although often this seems an irrelevant question, it sometimes leads to startling discoveries. How much modern theory owes to de Broglie's suggestion that, if wave phenomena are intelligible in terms of corpuscular, perhaps corpuscular phenomena might be intelligible in terms of wave phenomena. This is to proceed from the supposition of similarity and inversion. Schrödinger, took this seriously and tried to set up the possible wave motions for corpuscles. The predictions concerning spectral emissions from various elements previously not reducible to any accurate mathematical formula were startlingly precise.

Similar suggestions have been behind the positing of antimatter and, in general, similarity and bipolarity in nature, or, more generally, symmetry. Of course, integrity, harmony, and clarity have always been observed in organic nature and have provoked quasi-aesthetic reactions. Organic nature is thus a sort of aesthetic experience objectivized.

I would like to argue here that the reason for the impinging of the aesthetic upon scientific theory, is the grounding of all human experience, properly so-called, in imagination. And I would add that the fundamental perception of imagination is magnitude and time. Through these secondary sensibles for the external senses, but primary for the internal, all rational insight occurs. Thus, through magnitude and time, the possibility of intellectual perception is set up in inner sensibility. Magnitude and time create the terms of the relations which the intellect then actually relates.

But magnitude is the basis for this as the effect of quantity upon the quantifiable thing—the quantified thing in fact, which is the object of human experience. If we suppose that quantity is the prime root of relation and that relation is the prime object of human thought, then it follows that quantity lays the groundwork for human thought. Human thinking is the perception of the relations in the objective world which quantity basically grounds.

Thus, through its divisibility and then actual division, it sets up multitude and thus opposes sensed thing to sensed thing and qualities in sensed things which are, in themselves, not opposed, but become opposed, that is related one to the other. The human intellect then grasps these as similar or dissimilar, that is to say, relates them.

The prime mental function which gives rise to mathematics is thus the same one which gives rise to art—the division of the divisible. The division of three-dimensioned quantity gives rise to the perception of the limits of division—of the indivisible terms within the divisible whole, and these, then reversed, "generate" lines and figures and solids and with them the science of geometry. The division of the undivided divisible—the unit which classical thought therefore considered quite critically not to be itself a number but the origin of all number—gives rise to arithmetic. Contrary to Kant's claim, this has nothing to do with time. But it is not to my point here to enter into the philosophy of mathematical science or the nature of number, but simply to show one reason for the natural interrelation of mathematics and art. Both divide up the divisible and relate parts to wholes.

Of course, from that point on they depart company. Mathematics is then interested in rational and universal relations existing between the parts, whereas art is not. And art is interested in the qualities in the parts, whereas mathematics is not. For this reason, the divisions which mathematics makes can be reduced to universal formulas, but those of art cannot. The relations which art sees are therefore dimly intelligible, whereas those of mathematics are clearly intelligible.

This is well-known to every practicing artist. The artist distinguishes clearly between the geometrical center and what he often calls the "optical" center in the placing of a part within the whole of a canvas. He is aware that what seems to the aesthetic eye as the proper center does not prove to be so if the compass and the ruler are applied. The artist must in fact make an effort not to be trapped by the compass and the ruler. The aesthetic center is somewhat higher than the true geometrical center. This means to me that the aesthetic eye approximates but does not identically agree with the geometrical. This can and should be extended to the aesthetic perception of the center of gravity and all analogates.

This has to mean that reason, working with mathematical precision, seeks centers and relationships in the divided quantity of the divisible, but that reason, working in the realm of the aesthetic, moves off from this and therefore into the realm of the less precisely understood relationality.

From this, one may conclude that relation—here the relation of the center to the periphery or the general relation of similarity—has two extremes in its intelligibility. It has the precise extreme of the mathematical and the only approximate extreme of the aesthetic.

Thus, one could say that relation mediates between precise reason and imprecise sense impression—in fact, ties sense impression to reason. But to develop this further would take us *ex professo* into the philosophy of relation. It suffices for our purposes here in the theory of art to note the phenomenon—that is to say, that relation mediates between reason and the sensed. The artist is concerned with the sensed extreme of the mediation, and the mathematician with the rationally precise extreme. This is why the artist moves away from the compass and the ruler and from mathematical precision, but at the same time cannot critically flee from reason.

The relationality which the artist intuits is dim but there. The aesthetic is not beyond the realm of reason, but at its fringe, where it just touches the potentially intelligible. Those modern artists who have therefore sought to make their art irrational have simply not understood its true nature. Those who have tried to ground it in will and choice to the exclusion of reason have likewise misunderstood its nature. Reason and will and sensed experience and imagination and passion all go together to form parts of a whole. And the parts—the true parts—of a whole cannot be in opposition. They stand off from one another within the whole, but they do not contradict one another or destroy one another. To conceive of them as if they did is to misconceive them and to destroy the very essence of art.

By the anchoring of the aesthetic in the mathematical, I want therefore to mean not that the aesthetic is a deduction from mathematical theory, but that the two have common roots in the very nature of reason and sense experience and that they instinctively see this. The aesthetic gets closer to the sense pole of these roots and sees relationality more dimly, and because of this cannot universalize. The mathematical abstracts from the sense pole—the diagram, which aids the mathematician in getting into his thought, and cripples its development if he pays attention to its sensible qualities. The artist must get at the relation insofar as it is in the sensed content, but the mathematician insofar as it abstracts from it. The mathematician may etch a circle in bronze, but he is not then concerned with the "bronzeness" of the circle, but its "circularity" in abstraction from the bronze. The artist is concerned with the bronzeness of the circularity as an object of sense experience.

Thus, both mathematics and art deal with the divisibility of the divisible and with the relations which follow from this. They are both therefore in touch with the primary element of inner sensation and with relationality insofar as it is involved in this. This element, as I have argued, is that of magnitude, not of time. The addition of time and of quality moves aesthetics closer to the sciences beyond mathematics so that it can then be compared to "empirical science"—which we have already partly noted—and to philosophy as such.

What is characteristic of reason in its scientific use is that it touches upon the object "in itself." But in physics, it reaches down to the sensibly given object; in mathematics, to that object insofar as it is in imagination; and in metaphysics, to the same object as it is purely and simply in intellect. That is why Plato had grave questions about the status of physics and why he saw mathematics as the intermediate science, but metaphysics as the divine science.

Artistic activity, as part of this whole, must therefore relate to all three. And I have therefore argued in this chapter about how it touches on mathematics, and I have also indicated certain ways in which it touches upon physics. In a sense, it makes the thing which the physicist studies. And the artist has the feeling of coming to know the matter upon which he works through the very activity of art. There is also the experience in art, both as produced by the artist and as viewed by the non-artist, or at least by some other artist than the one who produced it, that it conveys a metaphysical sense of being and of life. Anyone who has painted a mountain feels that through this experience he possesses the mountain and through that possession has insight into being. One who hears the late quartets of Beethoven senses that something equivalent in its own way to a profound metaphysics is being mediated by them. I would argue also, along the same line, that all of the phenomena of reason are found in their own way in art—not merely the phenomenon of conceptualization as this is specifically found in the perception of relation. Thus judging and reasoning too are found in it, just as they are in mathematics.

Let me now introduce the imagination content of time. I have already said that this is not, contrary to Kant's position, the root of number. But time too is divisible, just as magnitude is. And just as magnitude is the volume of body, so time is the "volume" of local motion of body. As a sort of volume, it is thus divisible, and the mathematics which properly originates through the division of magnitude can then be applied to it. Thus, time also becomes the classical "measure of motion." And its division becomes available for art. Music makes use of this, dividing up time into parts and adding qualities to the parts through sound. Thus comes measure and meter and harmony, but also, as in the graphic arts, cacophony. There is, in this phenomenon in music, something of the "optical center" phenomenon for the visual arts. The aesthetic for the ear is rooted in but not tied to the precise mathematics of tonal ratios.

As much can be said, obviously, for the literary arts. Meter and tone enter into their essential considerations qua aesthetic. The very word "poetry," as Aristotle points out, came from the understanding of the poet as a maker of meters. In this way, then, art is continuous with the imagination and with mathematics and with all science and action.

CHAPTER 12

The Convergence of Artistic Wholes

Kant reintroduced modern thought to the classical notion of the teleological through the "ideals of pure reason." He did this, of course, from a totally different point of view and for different purposes than the classical. But, regardless of this, he was still in harmony with an ancient idea and was, in fact, rediscovering it for himself through premises which he took from apparently antithetical modern thought.

Thus, he pointed to the fundamental principle which we have been proposing—that any specific work of art is a relation of parts to a whole, which whole itself relates beyond to other wholes and eventually to the absolute whole, which is self-possession. This end is mediated through the endeavor to possess the world through "making" it, and through this making possess God as the absolute through the medium of making. The making, of course, touches directly upon the world and only indirectly upon the self and upon God.

Thus, in the life work of a great artist, each production is part of this totality and moves toward it. And in this way, through an immediate making, the artist aims at an eventual doing—that doing which is possession of the self through the world of God through both.

Thus, just as there is the growth of the thinker and the growth of the moralist, so also there is the growth of the artist. And, just as the growth of the thinker is through deeper insight into the intelligibility of the world and through that of the self, so the growth of the moralist is through greater rule of self which is growth in freedom and domination of the world through this. And the growth of the artist is through the making with the world of aesthetic wholes whose interconnection aims at an absolute whole.

As we will see James Joyce took this quite literally. The "making with the word" thus became for him sacramentally efficacious. Through art, he sought a "quasi-sacramental" redemption. Of course, he was drawing upon his Catholic tradition which understood and still understands the Eucharist as an efficacious sign. And he was following closely in the steps of the interpretation of this efficacity which Aquinas classically formulated. It was more than moral efficacity. It was also real physical efficaciousness. It was real transubstantiation which makes Christ really to be present through the consecratory act. The eating of the product of this realizing activity, then, really transforms the believer. Grace divinizes. And the sacramental activity through which grace is produced, *makes* a human being divine. This understanding brings us, however, into the theology of art.

From the purely philosophical point of view, which is also a "natural theology" in the presuppositions of this philosophy of art, the convergence of the aesthetic wholes is toward the total possession of the natural self. This must not be conceived of as a mosaic-like augmentation of any one whole by the addition of others, but a penetration in depth. The succession of the "wholes" is such as to exhaust more and more the intelligibility of the ultimate whole. If this is not the case, the work of the artist is moving on the sphere which surrounds the center, rather than moving in toward the center itself. The work then remains equidistant from the center. The work of the profound artist, on the other hand, moves progressively in toward the center. Its successive states are more like a contraction of a spherical surface which terminates in concentration at the center.

There is a parallel to this in the life of virtue. In the growth of virtue, one comes closer and closer to the positing of that final act through which ultimate happiness would be seized upon, if this were possible. That is the sense of the growth. But, of course, the ultimate act which seizes upon happiness—upon self and God—is not possible to unaided human activity. It is the "gift of the gods," as Aristotle says, or, in the case of the imperfect happiness of this life, either the effect of divine intervention or of chance—chance at least with respect to the human capacity. The human capacity is therefore of necessity only that of posing all those actions which tend toward the ultimate, but not of posing the ultimate itself unaided. The same can be said of the movement of art to the same goal.

Sin in the moral movement is the seeking of the intermediate as if it were the ultimate. It is therefore a seeking of the less-than-self—a choice and an intention not fully to actualize the human potential. The convergence of actions is then toward a false self. And the consequence of this is alienation from the true self, from which the movement starts out and toward which it naturally tends.

In a similar way in art, the convergence of the aesthetic wholes may be to some aesthetic intermediate which, as such, truly is a potentiality, but not the ultimate one. This introduces alienation into the aesthetic. Artists thus come to be at odds with the source of their artistic drive and with the "demon" which beckons them on. What is seized upon is indefinitely removed from the true demon and the removal—the holding off and the alienation—is the work of artists themselves. There is inner war rather than peace. There is a sense of dispossession rather than of possession. Chaos replaces order. Fragmentation replaces unity. This situation can be represented in Figure 12-1.

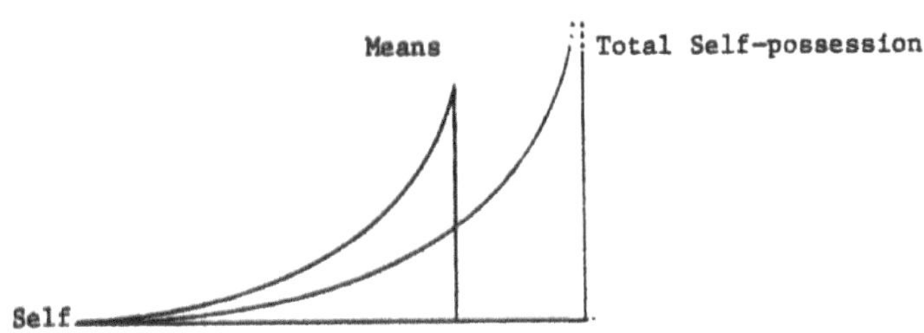

Figure 12-1

The representation is linear. The ego is at the beginning and at the end. The ideal curve of the movement toward the self, since the human capacity can pose any action short of the ultimate, is an asymptotic approach to the ultimate. The factual curve of action which falls short of this is, as it were, a complex asymptotic movement toward an intermediate. The intermediate can, in fact, be reached, since it is an intermediate. But, if it is, then it tends to be replaced by another intermediate, and this indefinitely. Or even the piling up of such intermediates may be of such a nature as to circle around the intermediate which is truly intended, but of which the artist or moralist is unaware. The parallel between this and the Freudian analysis should be obvious.

At all events, the intermediate becomes not a point of transition to the ultimate, but a point of impediment holding back from movement to it. This creates the feeling of alienation. The demon at the end then becomes evil. It beckons on, but the artist or the moralist resists. Thus, ego as a source of drive and ego as end of drive are pitted against each other. The self is split.

For this reason, Aquinas can speak of the life of advancing virtue as a movement from multiplicity to unity, and the life of viciousness as a movement from unity to multiplicity. The true intelligibility of the self is rendered radical unintelligibility. And the true being of the self—its identity—is shattered into unrelated atoms.

Thus, the self at the beginning and the self at the end are, at least in the sense of the thrust and the consequent phenomenological analysis of the results, shattered. For the artist, the moralist, and the philosopher/scientist, the beginning of all things becomes senseless, purposeless atoms, and they too are the end. It all begins in chaos and ends in chaos. Yet the very engine of the thrust and its sense are at odds with this interpretation. No one with any critical acumen or even simple humanity can mistake this. Hence, the many movements, in the chaos of the contemporary scene, toward unity. And, when western European thought, forgetful of its classic past, cannot find the principle of the unity within itself, it seeks for it in eastern thought.

Sometimes, when morality and science seem helpless to provide this, even the scientist turns to art, as if it could supply the lack. Thus, Gell-Mann named his ultimate particles "quarks" because he like the aesthetics of the name when he read it in Joyce's *Finnegans Wake.* And John Updyke somewhere speaks of the transition: "priest-teacher-artist." The forgetting of Plato, repeated in Heidegger's theme of the forgetting of being—rather than the bringing back by memory of what once was—are themes; but this recourse to art rather than remembrance of things past is certainly a characteristic of the contemporary mind. It is as if the contemporary mind seeks to replace lost moral values with aesthetic ones. And the aesthetic ones are precisely those which bring order and sense and goodness to reality.

But art is in the same position as morality and science (in which I include philosophy, since I take science in the classical sense, still retained in the German). The diagram which I have offered for the situation of the "sinful human being" applies equally to the "sinful" artist and the "sinful" scientist. All, in fact, seek the ultimate in the intermediate. And since, as I presuppose, there is no choice concerning the ultimate, this sets nature at war with nature ,and self at war with self.

The ideal would be for the growth of the whole person in each case to be by way of concentration of spheres of activity so that all would terminate in the infinitely condensed center. The ideal would be for all three movements to occur at the same time and to follow their natural pace and to relate naturally one to the other as parts of an organic whole.

If we now make an abstraction and consider only the movement of the artistic into the ideal, and if we take, as a presupposition, that it is the making of the aesthetic whole/parts relations, then we must conclude that its progress would be by convergence of wholes, by concentration of wholes. And, if the life of the artist followed this ideal path, it would be of this character. And it would therefore be progressively more human and, beyond that, more personal. And the personal would draw from the social (human cooperation), just as science and morality draw from the social.

But we are here at the point where philosophy, just as morality and art, come to despair. We are at the point which magical-sacramental and, for much the same reason, Gnostic practice, claim to have the answer. We have run up against an apparent possibility of human action, and what should be the case, but what is in fact not the case. What should be is not so. The good are not rewarded nor the evil punished. Growth in knowledge does not lead to greater possession of self, but to intensifying alienation from self. The very thing which should, by its nature, produce unity, in fact divides. Art falls into the same pit. And, therefore, humanity at large fears the scientist, scorns the artist, and derides the moralist. Inductive experience convinces the masses that there is no way out of this impasse through any of these great human channels. Magical-sacramental religion and the religion of the book tell us that the only way out is through "salvation" by special divine intervention whose actuality is believed in by a belief which is itself a divine free favor.

It is interesting, for those who are willing to recall the past, to remember the difference in this between Aristotle and Plato his teacher. Plato adopted the "magical-mystery" solution. But Aristotle always hesitated to do this and tried as best he could to find a way out through reason. This remained his endeavor to the last. He judged to the end that the myths encapsulated reason, and in his last days he paid a final tribute to them. He said that the more he was alone and by himself, the more he loved the myths. That might seem a strange statement from a man who in many ways has exemplified philosophical reason to the classical and medieval and modern world—at least to one who does not understand what Aristotle means by "myth." But it is in fact a final rejection of the mystery religion "salvation" solution. Human beings should not need salvation. They should be able to break through to the end by reason itself and by morality and art. Let this serve as an introduction to the final chapter, in which I will discuss James Joyce.

CHAPTER 13

James Joyce: Salvation Through Art

Usually, when the aesthetic philosophy of Joyce is discussed, reference is made to his love for Aquinas and to his acceptance of Aquinas' definition of art as that which, when seen, pleases (*quod visum placet*). Perhaps somewhat less frequently, reference is made to Joyce's use of Aquinas' designation of the properties of the beautiful as integrity, consonance, and radiance. Even less frequently—nearly not at all in these discussions—is reference made to Aquinas' definition of art as that which lies at one extreme of reason. This definition can be thought of as the Platonism of Aquinas, although he would not have seen it as a Platonism antithetical to Aristotle—for him, *the* philosopher.

Yet, it is this definition which most closely matches the sort of literary endeavor in which Joyce engaged. I have not been able to find it explicitly mentioned in his works, and it may be that he picked it up by a sort of intellectual osmosis, since he read so assiduously in Aquinas. But it is the definition which most closely fits his artistic accomplishment.

Something akin to it does occur in Plato, and Maritain makes reference to this. But, in Plato, the "fringes" are an instrumental use of reason by the gods such that the person under the influence of this use seems to exceed reason. Plato refers to it therefore as a *mania*—an excess of reason or a going beyond reason. Aristotle refers to the same phenomenon as *enthusiasm* and understands it in exactly this same way. And what he has to say about enthusiasm is taken, lock, stock, and barrel, into Aquinas' doctrine of the "gifts of the Holy Spirit." These are for him the basis of mysticism and, through his great influence, they entered into Rheinland mysticism in Eckhart, Tauler, and Suso.

One could argue that, for Plato, this excess of reason truly is a going beyond by a higher faculty, but, certainly in Aquinas and also in Aristotle, it remains within the realm of the rational. In the human mind there is, for both, no higher principle than reason.

At all events, it could be said that Joyce, having abandoned the "theological excess" of Aquinas' definition, then tries to occupy the same territory with the "poetic excess." He thus tries to seize upon the object of theology by art. If the theological excess is ultimately the conjunction of the self with self and with God, then the artistic is the same, but it is achieved through the character of the artistic in itself. The demon achieves the consummation which the sacramental ritual promises.

Joyce sees this effort as creative in a sense paralleling the divine creativity of Genesis. He likes to use the words of the priestly account of creation. There is a line in *Finnegans Wake* which brings this out well and also shows the continuity between the poetical devices of Joyce and those native to Celtic poetry and ornamentation: "This exists that is its after having been said we know...." Through a series of rearrangements and analyses, a possible genesis of the line itself can be seen:

1. "This exists, that is (its having been said) (we know)"

2. "(we know) (this exists) (that is) (after) (its having been said)"

3. "after (its having been said), /then/ (this exists), (we know)"

The movement from "let there be light and there was light" to this seems obvious. It seems, then, to say that we (the artistic self) know—that is to say, the reality which we assert is actualized by that fact— that, having said "let there be light," there is then light. We are conscious of ourselves, in other words, as the God of Genesis was conscious of himself as bringing about the existence of light through the power of the word.

There is arrogance in this interpretation of artistic activity on the part of Joyce. But there is also something clearly Roman Catholic in it and something at least osmotically Thomistic. One could say that it is a perverted Roman Catholic and Thomistic sensibility. But both perversions, if they really are such, could only have their roots in sacramental Catholicism and in Aquinas' understanding of the use of symbols in both extremes of the rational. The use of symbols in the middle reaches of reason—the use, let us say, of metaphors—is a way in, but, from that point on, an impediment to reason. Reason must abstract from the symbolization of the rational to confront the rational in itself. Inability to do this is what makes the acquisition of mathematical or metaphysical skills impossible. Hence, the rejection of the Platonic metaphors in "serious" thought by Aristotle. But, while this rejection is necessary for serious rational thought in the middle realm of reason, it is impossible at the fringes of reason. There, reason must use metaphors to get at the object at all. Aquinas is of the opinion, as we noted before, that this is because of the faint intelligibility of the *per se* (poetical, he would say) and of the too powerful intelligibility of the theological. In both cases, the object can be got at only through a medium, and that medium is the metaphor.

John of the Cross uses a similar device, obviously under the same inspiration, in the presentation of his mystical teachings. He first composes a poem—a brief stanza—and he then presents a rational theological exposition of the "meaning" of the stanza—as if to say that he is going to reach out and possess it by the infra-rational and by the rational.

What is interesting in this, aside from its relevance to Aquinas' definition of art, is its integrity. John of the Cross has had the mystical expedience and can communicate it beyond the upper limits of reason by metaphor—aside from this, he speaks of it as ineffable, meaning not directly communicable in rational concepts. The metaphor is the "dark night in which the soul goes forth secretly to meet the beloved one and finds the beloved one and gives rest to him on the breast with the sound of the gentle wind among the cedars." This is a metaphor and a narrative, but also a poem, so that the sounds of the words taken in themselves have aesthetic value: "*En una Noche obscura.*"

The comparison between this and the words of Christ to the effect that the kingdom of heaven is like a mustard seed is obvious. Christ sometimes brings the metaphor into the strictly rational area, and there explains what is acceptable and necessary conduct, granted the metaphor. The disciples then amusingly praise him for no longer speaking in parables. But Christ composes no poetry—at least we have no direct evidence of this, although the parables might have had poetical structure in their original form.

John of the Cross therefore sweeps the entire spectrum of Aquinas' understanding of reason and its possibilities. Dante puts into poetry substantially Aquinas' view of the human situation, granted Christ and salvation. But he understands what he does as just that. Joyce, on the other hand, seems taken with the idea of having poetry occupy the upper ground. The idea, if that is truly what he intended, is blasphemous to a believing sacramental Christian. But the blasphemy seems to intrigue Joyce. It might be too harsh to say that he intended the blasphemy to wound a Roman Catholic conscience or to get back at what he did not like in his Irish Roman Catholic roots. A gentler understanding of what he was about as a venture would be based upon a compelling thought not at all theoretically foreign to the theology of Aquinas: Suppose that we were all in the condition of Jesus—Aquinas holds this to be in principle possible—but *de facto* then the apparent arrogance of Joyce would be not arrogance, but truth. We would all of us say "let there be light" and, from that saying, "light would be."

To heighten the sense of this consideration, let us conceive of Christ as the *realized metaphor* and of the sacramental system as itself also the realized and realizing metaphor through continuity with Christ. Then the metaphors become not the expressions of the man, John of the Cross, endeavoring to communicate a ineffable experience, but the words of the man/God not only communicating an experience of a truth or a knowledge, but bringing them into being by the mere speech or the symbolization. The speaking, then, of this subject creates, transforms, and realizes. It is being-making and salvific.

Many artists and writers have toyed with this idea. Eric Voegelin attributes something of this to Hegel, looking for the Zauberwort. Thomas Mann, in the short story *Mario and the Magician* and in *Death in Venice*, but most markedly in the *Dr. Faustus*, also plays with the idea. Heidegger certainly also was intrigued with the "magic" of the word. It is an idea which entered general human culture indefinitely many years ago. One could conceive of Joyce as giving it a special concretization through his Roman Catholic roots. The subject then speaking, in *Ulysses* and in *Finnegans Wake,* is the man/God—the Christ—who is the writer.

JAMES JOYCE: SALVATION THROUGH ART

Even the scatology and the apparently deliberately offensive statements in Joyce make sense in terms of this. God made the possibilities for these and allowed them to occur, and they are history. It is as if Joyce, by offensively (especially to the Roman Catholic Irish countryman of his day) stating this, wished to bring to consciousness (at least of that audience) that God is not as simple as he is sometimes presented. He is the Lord of history in which all of this occurs.

It seems to me that the notion of the creativity of the word and its possible appropriation by the artist is more easily assimilated in magical-sacramental religion than in religion purely of the word. Religion purely of the word finds it difficult to identify the speaker—the artist—with the divine. But religion of the effective symbol, in which words are formal, finds this relatively easy. And, when that religion takes the eucharistic words as transformative, so that God is not merely understood to be effectively in the bread and wine when they are consumed—as he is understood to be in the waters of Baptism when they wash—but to be really there even when they are not used. They are the body and blood of the Christ. If this is so, then the sort of thought which one could attribute to Joyce becomes more easily understandable.

Harnack, commenting on this and referring to the special sacramentality in the theology of Aquinas, and particularly to his doctrine of transubstantiation, remarks that this is the only way to go—the most logical consistent and the most thoroughgoing for one who embraces sacramental Christianity. Of course, he did not think that this was the Christianity which Jesus himself taught, but that is not my point. God said "let there be light and there was light." Jesus said "let this bread be my body and let this wine be my blood" and the bread was then his body and the wine was then his blood. The direct order would be, to the bread, "be my body," and, to the wine, "be my blood." And, if the subject saying these words was God, then the words were effective.

We should add to this another theme in Aquinas which fell away in late medieval Nominalism and in the Reformation, but was strong in the Greek fathers. This is the theme of divinization. Grace does not leave everything simply as it is, but really transforms the human person. Graced humanity is more than human. The realism of this was at the heart of the mystical theology of Eckhart, Tauler, and Suso. Graced humanity, then, does more than ungraced humanity for which the Ten Commandments would provide at least an elemental code of action. Graced humanity can do the things of God—can act like God—can move mountains. Aquinas grounds this conviction on the creativity of the love of God. If, humanly speaking, God changes from not loving us in the sense of grace—and here Aquinas is careful to assert this possibility in order to preserve the divine freedom in bestowing grace—to loving us in the sense of bestowing grace upon us, then we are ontologically altered. We become gods. We become the trinitarian God.

The extreme of realism of this theme is spelled out in detail in the words of John of the Cross. As divinized, he is the Trinity, and therefore he breathes the Spirit within himself which the Father and the Son breathe in the radical Trinity. It would be difficult to imagine such language in any other than extremely realistic Thomistic thought. Grace is not simply the overlooking or the forgiving of sin, but the creative alteration of human nature.

A Thomist can recognize all of this in Joyce, the artist, but, without some endeavor to place it in context, may take it as arrogance, pure and simple. But, placed in context, it no longer seems like a simple arrogance, but a complex arrogance based upon a real struggle to understand his own human situation through continuity with his Roman Catholic roots and through the understanding of those roots which he was able to wrest from his life-long reading of Aquinas. This reading did not make Joyce a professional scholar in the Angelic Doctor. But it certainly gave him themes and understandings which help to explain his otherwise puzzling writings.

Let me close by saying that I have come over into the realm of the theology of art and therefore should not pursue the point further within the context of a discussion of the philosophy of art. But my purpose in taking this direction was to honor a great writer whose centenary occurs in 1982, and whose Celtic psychology is echoed in my own—I therefore understandably vibrate strongly to it.

Shortly before his death, in a conversation with a friend in Lausanne, Switzerland, he is said to have remarked that, without the help of "my Irish Saint" (Patrick, whose stories and life are interlaced in his works), he could not have finished *Finnegans Wake.* May he have found by now what he sought to seize upon through art in *Ulysses* and that last work: the final meaning of the human situation and peace.

SELECTED BIBLIOGRAPHY

Aristotle. *Poetics* . With an Introductory Essay by Francis Fergus. New York: Hill and Wang, 1961.

Burckhardt, Titus. *Sacred Art in East and West: Its Principles and Methods.* Translated by Lord Northbourne. London: Perennial Books, 1967.

Cary, Joyce. *Art and Reality: Ways of the Creative Process.* Freeport, New York: Books for Libraries Press, 1970.

Claudel, Paul. *Poetic Art.* New York: Philosophical Library, 1948.

Collingwood, Robin George. *Essays in the Philosophy of Art.* Edited and with an introduction by Donagan. Bloomington, Indiana: Indiana University Press, 1964.

Coomaraswamy, Ananda Kentish. *Christian and Oriental Philosophy of Art.* Dover T 378 New York.

————. *The Transformation of Nature in Art.* Cambridge, Massachusetts: Harvard University Press, 1935.

Kennick, W., ed. *Art and Philosophy: Readings in Aesthetics.* New York: St. Martin's Press, 1964.

Langer, Susanne Katherina. *Reflections on Art: A Source Book of Writing by Artists, Critics, and Philosophers.* Baltimore: John Hopkins Press.

Malraux, Andre. *Museum Without Walls.* Translated by Stuart Gilbert and Francis Price. New York: Doubleday & Co., 1967.

Maritain, Jacques. Creative *Intuition in Art and Poetry.* New York: Meridian Books, 1955.

————. *The Responsibility of the Artist.* New York: Scribners, 1960.

Read, Sir Herbert Edward. *The Origins of Form in Art.* London: Thames and Hudson, 1965.

INDEX OF NAMES